SEA PRO

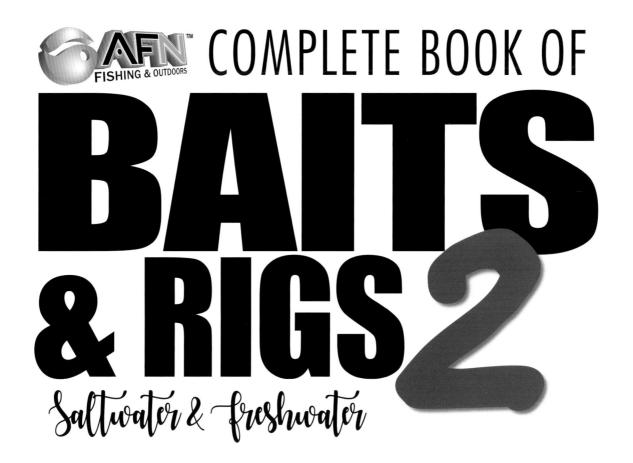

COMPLETE BOOK OF
BAITS & RIGS 2
Saltwater & Freshwater

TEXT AND ILLUSTRATIONS BY
Trevor Hawkins

EDITOR & CONSULTANT
Bill Classon

Introduction

BAITFISHING –FRESH AND SALTWATER

Long before the days of high-tech rods, braid lines, soft plastics and you-tube articles describing 'how to' and 'when to' it was often more common for beginner anglers to get started by fishing baits for some length of time before progressing onto lure or fly fishing. The progression to using artificials often came about once anglers became proficient enough with their own angling prowess to know where fish were, and what they would be feeding on at any given time, and to feel confident in their own fish catching abilities on any given water.

This 'apprenticeship' into fishing gave anglers a greater knowledge of the habits of their targeted species and taught them where fish were likely to be holding and what they would be feeding on. This knowledge of fish behaviour is the cornerstone of all fishing, no matter what species of fish you chase (fresh or salt) or angling method you use, and it is a mistake to rush through or ignore bait fishing as a legitimate angling method and treat it as simply a must do (or not do) stepping stone to other angling methods.

What many who don't, or won't bait fish miss, is the fun (and angling success) that can be had by refining and treating baitfishing as a legitimate angling method. In the hands of beginners and practised anglers, baitfishing, both static and dynamic can be a satisfying and very effective angling method, and worth taking the time to learn and enjoy.

This book sets out to give the reader a basic understanding of various baits, both fresh and saltwater, where to find, how to collect and handle, and how to rig those baits to get you started.

Good luck, Trevor Hawkins

Responsible and sustainable bait collection

As anglers who are using a natural resource to catch fish for sport or the table, we need to take our responsibility of only taking what we need for our immediate use seriously, we need to follow bait collecting and fishing regulations relating to the use of bait, live or dead, and return the bait collecting area back to the way it was originally as much as possible, for other anglers coming after us, and for the future propagation of those natural resources into the future.

Never collect bait on private property without permission from the landowner, and again, never take more than you need for your immediate use.

First published in 2019 by
Australian Fishing Network

AFN Fishing & Outdoors
PO Box 544, Croydon, VIC 3136
Tel: (03) 9729 8788
Email: sales@afn.com.au
Website: www.afn.com.au

This edition 2019. Reprinted 2023

Some basic observations

FRESH IS BEST

It doesn't matter whether you're drowning worms for stream blackfish or soaking a prawn to catch a black bream, fresh is always best when it comes to bait. The most successful bait fishers always prefer to use fresh local baits if possible. And while collecting your own bait can at times be a necessary evil, many recognised fishing regions and tackle shops have supplies of fresh local baits for sale.

Always try to transport and store your fresh bait so that it remains as fresh and lively as possible, so that it always presents most realistically to the fish.

Some baits that are very successful saltwater baits, can also be used in freshwater situations, several these come packaged and pre-frozen, and these are predominantly for saltwater fish, they often produce in lakes on trout. Frozen whitebait, mussels or pipis are good examples of these saltwater baits that will catch freshwater fish. They have a legitimate place in freshwater baitfishing, and shouldn't be overlooked, just the same as freshwater baits such as garden worms shouldn't be overlooked in saltwater applications at certain times.

OVERGUNNING

The most common mistake I see bait anglers making (fresh and salt) is using inappropriate sized tackle (hooks, line, sinkers and rods) for the fish being targeted and the area being fished.

Anglers presenting baits to fish should always try and do so in the most realistic fashion. Whilst there will always be 'silly trout' for instance that get caught by the anglers using gear more suitable for snapper in Port Phillip Bay, it is the thinking anglers who try and present baits in the most realistic way whilst using gear appropriate to the bait size, terrain being fished and size of fish being targeted that will consistently be rewarded with fish.

The bait angler chasing trout, redfin and yellowbelly in larger rivers and lakes can mostly get by with one rod size and weight and maybe a spare reel spool with a heavier breaking strain line for when rigs need to be beefed up for heavier baits and fish species.

These same freshwater outfits (lake, stream and larger rivers) are usually perfectly suitable for anglers who wish to switch over and do estuary and light saltwater fishing as well. So, the initial investment to rig appropriately for most freshwater and light saltwater species is usually modest. Many reels come with spare spools and these can and should be utilised by spooling with a line breaking strain in the next category up or down from what is on the other spool. Good line breaking strains for general trout, redfin and light native fishing might consist of one spool of 6 lb and the other of 10 or 12 pound. And these same lines are perfect for saltwater species such as bream, flathead, Australian bass and estuary perch and even Australian salmon and smaller snapper.

Contents

Artificial Power Baits 4

Bardi Grubs and Wood Grubs 5

Beach Worms 7

Blood Worms 8

Bread and Dough 9

Cabbage and Green Weed 10

Cockles and Pipis 12

Crabs 14

Crickets 15

Cunjevoi 16

Cut Baits 17

Cuttlefish 18

Estuary Shrimp 19

Freshwater Shrimp 20

Freshwater Yabbies 22

Garden Worms 26

Garfish 29

Grasshoppers 30

Herrings 31

Maggots 32

Minnows, Galaxids and Smelt 34

Mudeyes 36

Mullet 39

Mussels 40

Octopus 41

Pilchards 42

Pistol Shrimp 44

Prawns 45

Saltwater Yabbies 46

Sandworms 47

Scrubworms 48

Silver Whiting 50

Slimy Mackerel 52

Squid 53

Tuna 55

Whitebait 57

Yellowtail 58

Bait Jig Rigs 60

Bait Collecting Gear 62

ARTIFICIAL POWER BAITS

Artificial baits have become very popular with trout anglers in Australia. Whether you're just getting into baitfishing for trout, or a seasoned veteran, these baits at times can out-fish natural baits, or at the very least, compliment natural baits such as worms.

For many people the thought of impaling live baits such as worms or mudeyes can almost be a deal breaker when it comes to a day out fishing for trout. The introduction of artificial baits to catch trout has certainly eliminated the need to collect, buy or store live baits for single or multi day fishing trips.

While the baits may be artificial, the fishing is often just as productive as natural baits, and in many ways a lot more convenient.

PowerBait offers a clean and effective alternative to live bait and for those that want the convenience to go fishing at the drop of a hat or when travelling to areas where the collection and storage of live baits is problematic.

One of the main benefits of Powerbait is that it comes supplied in convenient air tight jars and is available in a multitude of colours and flavours, and what's not used

can be stored and used time and time again. Many anglers carry two or three different colours and flavours in their tackle box so that they have a selection to use because at times the trout prefer one colour or flavour over another.

These baits are extremely popular and productive when used to target rainbow trout in lakes.

PURCHASING

Artificial baits come in a variety of colours and flavours, and while it seems crazy to think that trout can and do favour one over the other at times, it does occur. The beauty of these baits is that a good variety can be easily carried, and is very economical and clean compared to buying or collecting and storing natural baits.

RIGGING

Applying power bait to your hook can be a little awkward at first as the consistency of the artificial is initially very sticky. I normally pinch out a manageable pee size piece from its tub and roll into a ball. I then slide it onto the leader immediately above the treble hook (or single

hook if you prefer) I've got rigged, I then slide it down over the hook so that it sits into the u-shaped sections of the treble hook allowing the three bends to sit around the outside of the power bait. Having the bait sit inside the treble assists when casting as it helps to hold the bait on the hook. You can also use single hooks with PowerBait, but if do want to use single hooks, then brands that have a wide gape to allow the hook point to remain clear of the bait when rigged.

One of the best features of these baits is that they float rather than sink like other baits, so that creates the opportunity to fish these in ways that can be very enticing, such as waving and swaying just off the bottom, or above weedbeds. They can

also be fished dynamically as well by the angler instead of the usual cast and wait method employed with other baits.

Fished below a standard running sinker from shore, these baits sway enticing mid water (depending on the length of your leader) and will hold in place in windy conditions unlike baits suspended under a float. With these running sinker rigs you can also run a combination of natural bait and artificial, or a double dropper rig with two different artificial baits while trying to find the most productive colour or flavour.

But as mentioned, these baits can also be fished dynamically by cast and retrieving, or drifting from a boat.

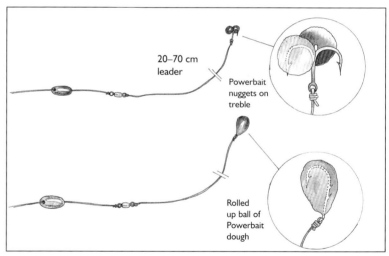

20–70 cm leader

Powerbait nuggets on treble

Rolled up ball of Powerbait dough

ARTIFICIAL BAIT RIGS

• Twin artifical bait rig is excellent over weed beds. Most artifical baits float and will suspend above the weed. Use light gauge hooks, so you don't weigh the bait down. Running sink should only be heavily enough to assist with casting.

If fishing sparsely weeded and rocky lake bed use twin rig with artificial bait and fresh/live bait combination. This set up is a great option to hedge you bets and cover both options

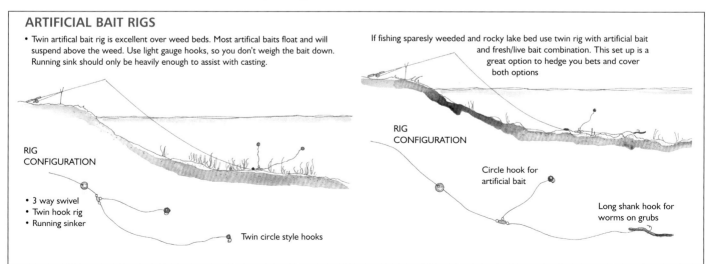

RIG CONFIGURATION

• 3 way swivel
• Twin hook rig
• Running sinker

Twin circle style hooks

RIG CONFIGURATION

Circle hook for artificial bait

Long shank hook for worms on grubs

BARDI GRUBS AND WOOD GRUBS

Grubs come in many shapes and sizes, but the two key grub baits are bardi and the wood grub. Both are the larval stage of moths, and in the case of the bardi grubs, the moths are extremely large and unmistakable for anglers frequenting our inland river systems.

LOCATING

Wood grubs are found burrowing in various tree types, the most common tree being the soft wooded kurrawong tree. Bardi grubs frequent the ground around and under the exposed roots of river redgums and grey box trees.

CATCHING AND HANDLING

Dead, fallen kurrawong trees are one of the best places to collect wood grubs, but other trees such as fallen wattles also give up these baits with the aid of an axe to split the wood and extract them.

Bardi Grubs take a little more effort to collect, but are very well worth it. By scraping away the soft top layer of grey powdery soil to reach the hard, dry clay layer, will reveal the bardi grub holes, a corkscrew type wire implement is then pushed down the hole and screwed slowly onto the bardi and then slowly withdrawn, hopefully with a bardi attached and not a cranky ground spider.

Grubs don't require special handling other than making sure you don't damage them during collection. They can be stored in a cool container in a mixture of sawdust or pieces of timber from with they were collected.

If the collected grubs are kept cool, they will often last several weeks before dying.

Bardi grubs can often be purchased at tackle shops and bait supply outlets in areas where these baits are most common and used, especially along our inland native fish rivers.

RIGGING

The best thing about using bardi grubs is that they are big and juicy, and once rigged onto a hook, they release enticing fluids that native fish, especially

BARDIES AS BAIT

When using a grub for bait, select a hook size that enables you to thread the grub so that the hook is well hidden with just the point and barb protruding from the head. When threading grubs onto a hook, begin at the tail and thread the shank to bring the hook point and barb out through the tough outer shell of the head. Thread the tail up over the eye of the hook and do a half hitch on the tail with the line. This will stop the grub from sliding down the hook and present it in a more natural, extended position. Because grubs can at times be difficult to find and expensive to buy, some anglers fix them to the hook using either a rubber band or Bait Mate. These methods keep the bait intact so if it goes uneaten it can be returned to the freezer and used next time around.

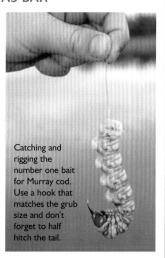

Catching and rigging the number one bait for Murray cod. Use a hook that matches the grub size and don't forget to half hitch the tail.

Above: A juicy grub rigged with a half hitch around the top and a small orange bead to assist with detection by fish.

COLLECTING BARDI GRUBS

Once you find your bardi grub hole insert a piece of wire, the end of which has been bent to corkscrew shape, then screw the wire over the grub and gently pull it out.

HOOKS FOR BARDI GRUBS

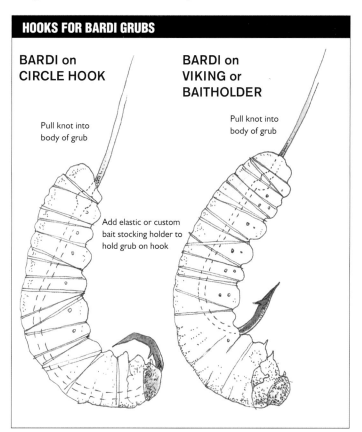

BARDI on CIRCLE HOOK

Pull knot into body of grub

Add elastic or custom bait stocking holder to hold grub on hook

BARDI on VIKING or BAITHOLDER

Pull knot into body of grub

OLD VS NEW

TRADITIONAL
Bardi Grub Rig
Running Sinker

1/4–2oz
Ball sinker

Quality swivel

10–20 kg
Mono

30–35 cm

1/0–7/0
Beak Bait Hook
or
1/0–8/0
French Viking Bronze

NEW STYLE
Paternoster Rig

Main line

Quality
swivel

Dropper Loop

20–25
cm

30–40 cm

Circle Hook
1/0–8/0

10–20 kg Fluorocarbon

Tear Drop Bomb
Sinker
1/4oz – 2oz or
required size

DROPPER LOOP

STEP 1
Form a loop

STEP 2 Twist cross-over
5–8 times

Pass loop through
central cross-over **STEP 3**

STEP 4
Pull up
slowly

Cut one side of finished
loop here to form single
dropper

STEP 5

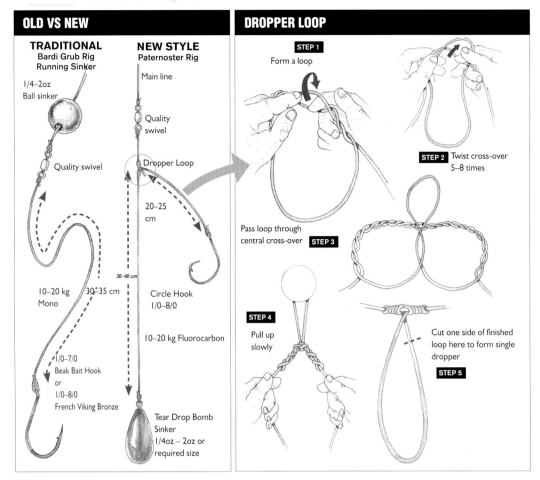

cod find irresistible. The best time to fish grubs is early morning, and late afternoon through to dusk. Rigging grubs is very like rigging earth worms, the key is to select a hook size that matches the grub, usually from 1-4, and completely impale the grub with the hook barb exposed. Some anglers thread the baits head first so that the head covers the hook eye and knot, while others do the opposite. Either method is successful, the main thing to do is to stop the bait being easily removed from the hook by fish, the leathery skin of the bardi is tough, but, wrapping the baited grub with bait elastic will hold the bait in place to avoid slipping up the line or down over the hook barb.

It's worth noting that bardi grubs are quite large and heavy, so unless you are fishing in strong currents or need to get a bait down quick, you can and should use as little weight as possible in lakes or slow backwaters and billabongs to enhance the natural presentation of these quality baits.

BARDI FACTS

The bardi Grub is also known as the witchetty grub and is a large, white, wood-eating larva of cossid moth , ghost moths and longhorn beetles. They belong to the Family Hepialidae Bardi grubs are usually found between 5cm to 10cm long, however larger specimens have been reported. The Bardi moth can lay in excess of 18,000 eggs and the larvae can take up to 3 years to mature and pupate traditional method.

Big cod just love big bardis.

PULLING GRUBS

The first catch begins with the bait and knowing how and where to get bardi grubs is a skill in itself. When looking for grubs along the Murray, select sugar gums that stand above the high water mark. Tell tale signs around the tree may come in the forms of old shells or holes left from last season's hatch.

With any, luck chipping away the first few inches of soil will reveal the grub holes. If the hole is silk lined and free of fine roots, then chances are there will be a grub inside. In some soils a hole that contains a grub will make a distinct popping sound when tapped with a finger.

There are two styles of bardi grub pullers used to extract the grubs.

The first works on the corkscrew principal where the wire is threaded into the grub. This is ok if you are going to use the grubs that day as it does damage them. The second, and my preferred choice, is the lasso style puller that's inserted down the hole and over the grub's head. The lasso is then pulled tight and the grub is drawn from the tunnel free of damage and can be kept alive for weeks in rolls of paper or boxes in the bottom of the fridge.

When you do find a good area of grubs don't dig them all, as when they hatch they tend to lay their eggs around the same area, so it is important to leave enough for next year's crop. It is also important to replace the topsoil from where you have been digging.

BEACH WORMS

Beach worms are best identified by the tiny legs extending out each side of their body. They are a very popular bait when chasing bream, whiting and several other estuarine or ocean beach species.

times. Many anglers simply buy fresh, live beach worms from bait supply shops, despite their expense.

The process requires the collector to walk the flats while allowing a smelly bait to attract the worms and bring them to

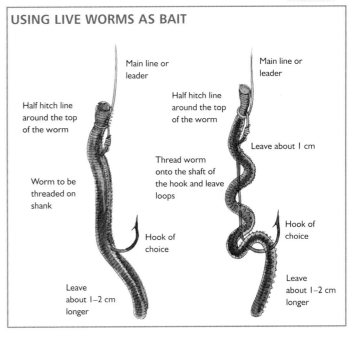

USING LIVE WORMS AS BAIT

Main line or leader

Half hitch line around the top of the worm

Worm to be threaded on shank

Hook of choice

Leave about 1–2 cm longer

Main line or leader

Half hitch line around the top of the worm

Thread worm onto the shaft of the hook and leave loops

Leave about 1 cm

Hook of choice

Leave about 1–2 cm longer

Fraser Island beach worming

LOCATING

Beach worms are found in the sloping sand areas along surf beaches from Queensland south to South Australia. They bury themselves in the wet sand along these beaches and feed on any food items that get pushed up over the sand with the wave movements. Ocean surf beaches usually have the best numbers of these worms and the ideal locations along these beaches are the long gentle slopes or sand spits leading into the water.

CATCHING

Beach worms aren't visible to the casual observer because, like pipis and crabs etc., they bury themselves into the soften wet sand and only come out if there is some food item for them to feed on. There is a real art to catching beachworm, and it can be very frustrating at

the surface. When the worm lifts out of the water, the deft bait collector garbs the arched wormed between the fingers and extracts it. Sounds easy, doesn't it?

In the book "How to catch Australia's favourite saltwater fish', Gary Brown shares the tips on how to go about collecting beach worms as shown to him by Alan Perry.

They are:

1 Use pilchards in a stocking secured to your ankle as the attractor bait.

2 Use a pipi that has been put in a stocking tied to your wrist for your hand bait.

3 Have the sun in front of you so you don't cast a shadow over where the worms are.

4 Make sure you don't grab at the worm until it has arched its back.

5 When closing your

forefinger against your thumb to make hold of the worm, make sure you have some sand between them to give a secure grip.

6 Once you have a worm between your forefinger and thumb, don't pull too hard, and take another hold with your other hand further down the worm.

7 Take your time.

HANDLING AND STORAGE

Beach worms can be frozen for use at a later stage, but these aren't nearly as productive as fresh worms. Fresh worms can be kept fresh immediately on capture by placing them in container of fresh seawater. After the collecting has finished, the collected worms can be placed into dry sand from the beach and wrapped in newspaper and kept cool.

RIGGING

Beach worms are quite tough and do stay on a hook for the most part. The key to rigging these baits is to realise that while they are relatively tough, they are slim and lightweight, and as such, to present in a natural manner to the fish, they should be thread onto light, fine gauge hooks. This is especially the case when targeting whiting and mullet.

Beachworms can be threaded straight onto a long shank hook, or by threading a longer piece of worm with the hook going in and out of the worm. Always leave a length of the worm at the head of the hook to allow for a half hitch to be taken to hold the worm in place, and leave a 40 to 50mm length of worm hanging from the hook bend to create and enticing moving section of worm to attract any nearby fish.

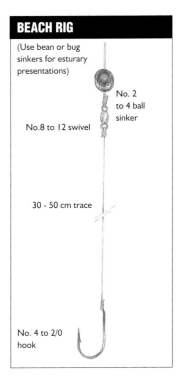

BEACH RIG

(Use bean or bug sinkers for esturary presentations)

No. 2 to 4 ball sinker

No.8 to 12 swivel

30 - 50 cm trace

No. 4 to 2/0 hook

BLOOD WORMS

While beach worms take some knack to collect, blood worms take hard work. They frequent mud banks and estuarine shorelines, were they live in in tubes and feed on any type of dead carrion that is available. They are big worms which can grow to a metre or longer, and their name comes from the blood like liquid that comes for their body when cut or placed on a hook.

is important to ensure you ARE permitted to collect bait in the area you intend to search, and if so, what if any limits there are on the amount of bait you can collect.

HANDLING AND STORAGE

The storing of blood worms can be problematical because they tend to go-off very quickly and you will end up with a smelly mess very quickly. Blood worms are very susceptible

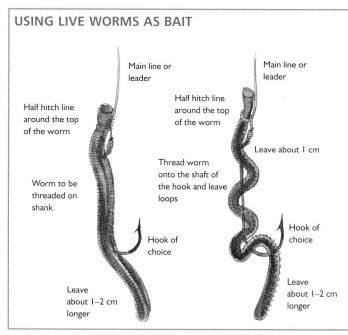

USING LIVE WORMS AS BAIT

Main line or leader

Half hitch line around the top of the worm

Worm to be threaded on shank

Hook of choice

Leave about 1–2 cm longer

Main line or leader

Half hitch line around the top of the worm

Thread worm onto the shaft of the hook and leave loops

Leave about 1 cm

Hook of choice

Leave about 1–2 cm longer

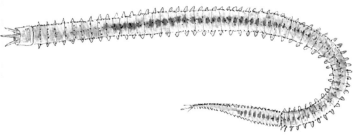

LOCATING

Blood worms are most commonly found deep in the mud of intertidal areas. Their range reaches from southern Queensland around to South Australia and can be found deep in the mud or sediment around shell beds, along the edges of weed beds and mangroves.

COLLECTING

A bait bucket, a shovel or pitchfork, and a preparedness to get covered in mud are the only prerequisites for collecting bloodworms. Once they have been found in an area, it is simply a matter of getting down to digging in the mud or grit to locate them. Often turning over rocks and logs etc. lying over the flats will show a worm or their tell-tale tube homes, and when these have been located, it's a good indicator there may be more worms in that location. Sounds easy, but it can be hard work at low tide up to your knees in mud, but it is worth it for a good haul of bait.

As with all bait collecting, it

to heat, so it is important to always keep them in the shade and later, if needed for another time, in the fridge at a cold temperature.

If possible take two containers, the first for collecting, and the second with clean seawater, upon digging a worm or two, or certainly sooner than later, wash the dug worms in saltwater to clean the 'gunk' off them, and then place in the container (preferably a cooler) with fresh seawater. They can also be stored in clean, moist but not wet, sand, but even then, they need to be stored in a 'fridge' like environment unless they are to be used within a few hours of digging.

RIGGING

Hooking and rigging blood worms is like other saltwater worms in that they can be threaded straight or bunched slightly. Small hooks are better than large ones so that the bait is not only conserved, but presents more naturally, and leaving a wiggling tail always

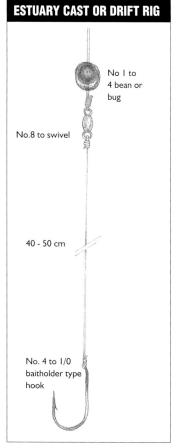

ESTUARY CAST OR DRIFT RIG

No 1 to 4 bean or bug

No.8 to swivel

40 - 50 cm

No. 4 to 1/0 baitholder type hook

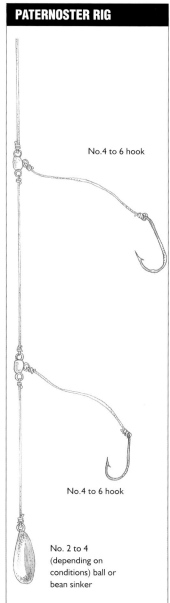

PATERNOSTER RIG

No.4 to 6 hook

No.4 to 6 hook

No. 2 to 4 (depending on conditions) ball or bean sinker

increases the baits appeal to the fish. Using baitholder hooks helps to prevent these worms sliding down the hook and bunching, and allows the use of smaller sections of these 'hard earned' baits when longer sections become scarce.

BREAD AND DOUGH

Bread is regularly used in berley mixtures and as a stand-alone bait to attract numerous species of fish. It is a very popular bait when targeting mullet, garfish, carp, roach, bream, blackfish, luderick, sweep, tommy ruff, trevally, slimy mackerel and yellowtail. Any fish that tend to mill about in schools can be attracted to an area with berley and then targeted using bread or dough baits.

BREAD BERLEY

Fresh white bread berley has been used for decades by anglers to attract and bring various fish species within range of their fishing rig. It is important when using bread as berley that it sinks down in the water column and doesn't just float on the surface. The trick is to break up the bread into a pulp, and mix in a little water so that the mixture can be squeezed to remove air and allow the mixture to sink and break up slowly as it sinks.

It is possible to add other items such as fish oil, mulched up pilchards or tuna to the mix as well to create an attractive oil scent from the berley.

Mixing i9n some sand or grit will also add some weight to allow the berley lump to sink. Berley cages that can be loaded with the bread mix can be useful to slow down the dispersal of the berley.

BREAD BAIT

Sliced or whole white bread seems to be more attractive to fish and hold together better than drier wholemeal and seed breads. Sliced fresh bread also allows you to use the tougher crust section on the hook and is a perfect width to go onto a hook.

Fresh white bread is soft and doughy and as such can be squeezed onto a hook in a tear

drop shape and will stay on the hook longer than staler bread that has lost its moisture and will crumble easily.

At times the targeted fish, often mullet and garfish won't be interested in a doughy mixture on the hook, and will only bite on un-kneaded fresh bread and when this is the case it often pays to use the crust section so it holds to the hook longer.

DOUGH

Dough is very popular (and cheap to make) bait that is very successful when targeting fish that tend to hang around jetties, rock walls and piers where people often feed swans, ducks and seagulls with bread. Fish such as mullet, garfish and bream get used to a semi regular feed of bread and a dough or bread bait, along with the use of s bread berley can be very productive in these areas.

DOUGH BAIT

You can make dough bait with a mixture of flour and water. The trick is to make the mixture to a consistency that will allow you to knead it onto a hook in a teardrop shape just as you do when using fresh white bread.

BERLEY RECIPE

An easy berley mix to make consists of chook pellets, tuna oil, bread, cat food and pilchard pieces. These should be mulched in a large plastic container and mixed in with water and allowed to soak for a day before use. Chook pellets and bread will soak the oil up. When this is done pour the berley into milk cartons and freeze.

When you go fishing remove one of the frozen berley blocks from the carton and put it into the berley bucket as you are travelling out. This will help to start the thawing process. An alternative is to place the frozen berley in an onion bag and leave it hanging over the side of the boat, but preferably off the bottom.

The simple process of lifting and dropping the bag while it is the water will start freeing up berley. The slow disintegration as it thaw will create a neat trail.

ESTUARY RIG

Pencil or quill floats are used when small baits need to be suspended in the water column for species including luderick, mullet, and trevally. The line below the float needs to be weighted to pull the float into a vertical position down into the water column with just a small portion of float visible above the surface.

The correct consistency will be firm enough to be handled and hold well on the hook.

MULLET, GARFISH YELLOWTAIL RIG FOR BREAD OR DOUGH

Berley float

DOUGH BREAD AND PUDDING RIG FOR BREAM, DRUMMER AND ROCKFISH

Small float

Ball sinker

No. 2 to 1/0 hook

2-2.5 metres 3kg line

No. 6 to 10 long shank hooks

BERLEY FEEDERS

Andy Teale is a coarse fishing guru (don't hold it against him, he is English after all) and he suggested using berley feeders to help attract whiting to my baits. The canisters are punctured with holes throughout the body that allows any berley stuffed inside to escape. The holes can usually be made smaller or bigger (like a cooking salt shaker) by turning the inner plastic tube. This effects how quickly the berley is dispersed into the water. I've found that rigging the canisters on the main line above the swivel is the way to go; however you can have them running directly above your baits. Some cages are weighted and have can be used in place of a traditional sinker but I personally prefer the unweighted variety. A simple berley mix can be made out of tuna oil soaked chicken pellets before being filled inside. When using berley cages it's good to concentrate multiple rigs in the same area so a good stream of berley is dispersed in a small area. Pre-soaking the berley mix will also help it to break down faster and fill the water column with a fine mist that won't fill the fish up.

CABBAGE AND GREEN WEED

Two different forms of seaweed used by luderick and rock blackfish anglers. Both fish species mentioned will also take prawns, crab, pipis and mussels etc. as bait, but the different forms of cabbage and weed mentioned here are traditional and reliable baits as well for these popular fish.

Green weed can be found growing on the rocks, stormwater drains, small streams and creeks. You can also use some in your berley.

LOCATING – GREEN OR BROWN CABBAGE

Cabbage is found between the low and high tide marks along sloping rocks, low edge areas, rock pools or channel markers. Intertidal zones, often where there is a good amount of wave action is often a prime area, and in certain places can grow in large clumps.

COLLECTING

During low tide, it is simply a matter of pinching off what's needed by pinching the cabbage at the base, between your thumb and forefinger and twisting off. This can then be used immediately or stored in some type of container for use elsewhere.

HANDLING AND STORAGE

Cabbage with stay fresh in a container for a day's fishing session, if kept moist with seawater so it doesn't dry out. If you've collected this bait for another fishing session in a day or so time, it can be wrapped in newspaper and stored in the veg section of your fridge.

WARNING

By its very nature, the collecting of these baits often requires anglers going onto wet and sloping rocks and areas at low tide that can be dangerous. Collecting bait in active surf or breaker zones should be totally avoided. Always keep one eye on sea to avoid rogue waves.

It does need to be kept moist though with a daily immersion in seawater. Rather than newspaper, it can be stored in the fridge in wet (seawater) hessian also.

RIGGING

Cabbage can be used for rock blackfish and luderick. For the generally smaller sized luderick, one leaf of cabbage or small amount of leaves on a size 8 or size 6 hook is used depending on fish size present. For rock blackfish, a larger cluster of leaves is threaded onto a size 2 to 2/0 hook.

To stop the weed from sliding down the hook shank, a half hitch is taken over the cabbage at the top of the hook. Many specialist 'weed' anglers have their own preferred method of folding or attaching cabbage to their hooks.

GREEN WEED

The number 1 bait for anglers chasing a feed of luderick in estuaries. Luderick anglers tend to be very particular with their specialist rigs and some even insist there are better species of green weed over others when chasing these prized fish. But for the most part, any green weed you collect will be acceptable so long as it is rigged and fished correctly. Saltwater

flyfishers are even starting to specialise in catching these fish using flies to represent the green weed. When collecting green weed for the first time, anglers should note not to collect the green slime weed found in freshwater gutters etc. as this isn't the correct weed and isn't attractive to the fish.

LOCATING – GREEN WEED

Green Weed (there are several different species all grouped together here) is generally found throughout intertidal zones of estuaries and can be gathered from rocks, rock pools, wooden structures and regularly in areas where natural or man-made drains flow into estuaries or tidal creeks.

COLLECTING

Depending where the weed is located, it can be gathered with your hands or some type of rake to entwine the weed and bring it in.

STORAGE

Green weed can also be kept in the bottom of the refrigerator. It can be frozen but it does tend to go slimy and is then best used as berley. A better storage method is to roll small amounts in newspaper and store in the vegie bin of the refrigerator, every few days

take the newspaper rolls with the weed inside and give a fresh soak in seawater before allowing the excess water to drain and placing back in the fridge.

Luderick are often encountered in areas where green weed is almost impossible to find, so planning a trip to those sorts of areas does require you to store good amounts of weed beforehand, in which case, getting a handle on a reliable storage method is very important.

RIGGING

Green Weed is best used sparse to avoid creating a large clump on your hook. A large or too short a lump will be difficult for the fish to get into their mouths. Creating a long and enticing weed bait is best done by taking a dozen or so individual strands of the weed and twisting or rolling them into a thing rope. This rope is then folded at its halfway point and placed on the line immediately above the hook eye. The two halves are then twisted down the line as shown in the illustration. It is important to leave a good length of weed hanging below the hook to allow the fish to try the bait before taking the baited hook itself.

Low tide reef access is a lure to anglers

DRUMMER

DESCRIPTION

The eastern rock blackfish (Girellidae) is often confused with the silver drummer (Kyphosidae). It is best distinguished by the dorsal spine counts of thirteen rather than eleven. The eastern rock blackfish are usually grey to black in colour, while the silver drummer can be a silvery grey or a grey/bronze. The upper side is often darker, and the fins are usually dark grey to black. The silver drummer will also have a silvery sheen and sometimes have pale stripes along its back. The western rock blackfish has a base colour of bluish black to brownish black that can occasionally be mottled with a white tinge.

GREEN OR BROWN CABBAGE

Where found: Is found between the low and high tide marks on the edge of low reef areas, sloping rocks boulders, channel markers and buoys and in rock pools.

Gather or catch it:

Use your thumb and forefinger to hold the cabbage at the base where it is attached to the rock and gently twist the cabbage off.

Storing: Once twisted off the rocks you can use it straight away, or store in a container for later use that day. If you are going to fish elsewhere in a couple of day's time, wrap the cabbage in newspaper and store in the bottom of the fridge.

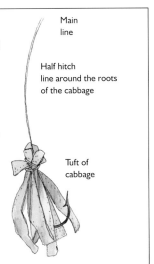

GREEN WEED AS BAIT

Where found: The green weed found in the estuaries is usually fine and very long, which has a thread like appearance. This seaweed bait can be found on submerged estuarine rocks, breakwall, wharves, bridge pylons, submerged logs and also over shallow flats that have been left dry for extended periods.

Gather or catch it: There is a small stormwater drain near my place that has an abundance of green weed and due to the depth of the water and the muddy bottom it can be hard to get. All I do is get my extendable pole that I use for the pool, fix a screw into the end of it and then poke it out into the water where the weed is. Then it is a matter of turning the pole around until you have twisted the weed onto the pole.

Storing: You can freeze the weed, but sometimes it tends to go a bit slimy when thawed out. Your best bet is to carefully wring out the excess water, wrap it up in newspaper and then store in the fridge for a few days. Once it starts to go a bit slimy you can always chop it up for berley.

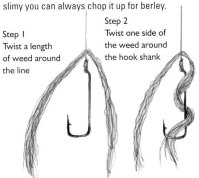

FLOAT FISHING FOR LUDERICK & DRUMMER

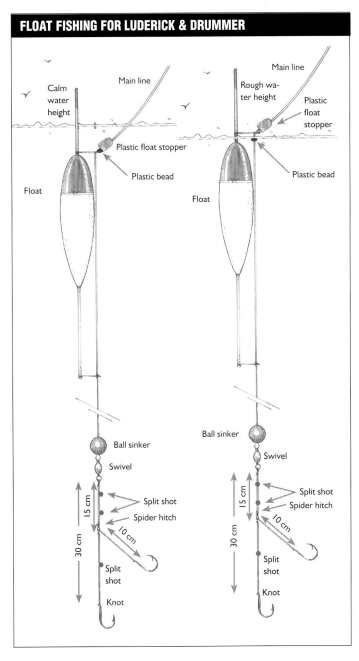

COCKLES AND PIPIS

The most commonly found and popular bivalve used by recreational anglers is the Pipi. Known by that name mostly in NSW, it is also referred to as Eugari in Queensland, Goolwa cockles in SA and cockles in Victoria. Whatever the name, these molluscs are a fantastic bait for many fish species in the surf and estuaries.

They range from Southern Queensland and southwards along the southern coast as far as the northern limits of the Coorong in Southern Australia.

They are a reasonably large bivalve mollusc growing to 7.5cm across the shell. They are triangular shaped without the obvious circular ridges of the true cockle.

Anglers should only take enough of these molluscs to cover their immediate fishing needs as they are susceptible to overharvesting. It's wise to check state regulations on where you can legally collect these baits and what the bag limit if any exists in the area you're collecting them from.

Pipis are the perfect bait when chasing whiting.

LOCATING

Pipis can be located along the eastern and southern state coastlines, usually along more remote areas of ocean beaches and where waves are pushing up and receding of the flatter sections of the sand, in areas not continually worked over by bait collectors. The lowest period of the tide generally offers the best chance to collect these baits. When you find one or two pipis you will normally find more, so search about until you come across good numbers. They can often be seen being pushed about by the waves washing over their positions as they live only a few centimetres under the sand.

COLLECTING AND HANDLING

Pipis are located by twisting your feet into the wet sand and feeling them. Stand in the shallow wash zone where the waves are lapping and twist both feet in the sand as the waves push in and out. If you feel anything hard under your foot, reach down and pick it up with your hands. Make sure you have

COCKLES

PIPIS

ESTUARY OR ROCK RIG

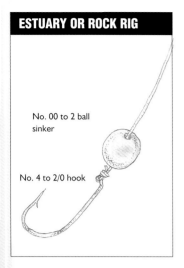

No. 00 to 2 ball sinker

No. 4 to 2/0 hook

PATERNOSTER RIG

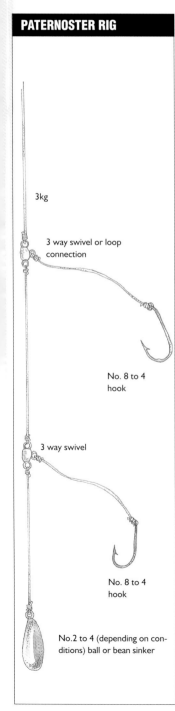

3kg

3 way swivel or loop connection

No. 8 to 4 hook

3 way swivel

No. 8 to 4 hook

No.2 to 4 (depending on conditions) ball or bean sinker

RUNNING SINKER RIG

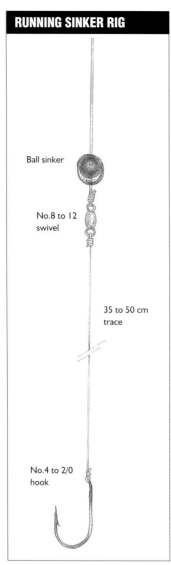

Ball sinker

No.8 to 12 swivel

35 to 50 cm trace

No.4 to 2/0 hook

Pumping the low tide for bait.

BERLEY

Crushed pipis make excellent berley, crushed so that they release their attractive scent and sink to the bottom, they attract many species of fish to the area you're fishing. One word of advice, don't overdo the amount of pipi berley you use though, 5 or so crushed shells initially is all that is needed to bring the fish around to start, and then one or two more crushed shells every 10 minutes should hold the fish in the berley area and feeding on your bait.

RIGGING

Pipis are very soft in texture, and as such can easily slide down and off the hook. To counter this, when the bait is removed from its shell, ensure that you leave the tougher part of the flesh attached so you can insert this area onto your hook first to help keep the bait on the hook when casting and being washed about in the water.

COCKLE

For all intents and purposes, cockles can be treated the same as pipis when it comes to fishing. They are just as popular as bait and used for the same species. Their range is from Albany in Western Australia to central NSW.

They differ in appearance in that their shell is heavier and ridged. They are also generally found away from the ocean beaches and wash zones and usually frequent the quitter water at the back of estuaries in sand and or sand and mud bottoms, they can be collected the same as pipis, although anglers tend to use pitchforks when collecting these baits.

some form of bucket or bait bag that allows you to store the collected bait as you move along the beach in search for more bait.

STORAGE

Pipis can be kept alive in bait wells or aerated buckets, and in wet sugar bags stored in cool shady areas.

As with all bait, fresh is best, however, if you do catch more than your immediate requirements, you can remove the flesh from the shell and lightly salt them, this will not only toughen the flesh up for fishing but allow you to keep them stored for a few days before they go off. Pipis can also be frozen to be used for bait at a later stage.

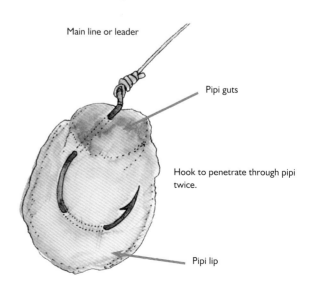

Main line or leader

Pipi guts

Hook to penetrate through pipi twice.

Pipi lip

CRABS

Crabs are one of the best, but possibly the least used baits in estuaries for some reason. They are easily caught and often produce better than average sized fish, which makes this lack of use even stranger. Casting unweighted small crab baits into likely bream areas is one of the best techniques for catching the big and wary specimens in fact.

If you start using them in estuaries you will regularly catch fish such as snapper, mulloway, bream, tarwhine, whiting and flathead.

LOCATING

Crabs of various species inhabit all saltwater environments, including rock walls, tidal sand and mud flats, mangroves, ocean rock pools. Using specific crabs that you locate around the areas you'll be fishing is often a good start as top what crab species to use for what fish.

Small specimens such as soldier crabs, black crabs and ghost crabs are popular when chasing fish such as bream, whiting, flathead, while larger crabs or sections thereof are

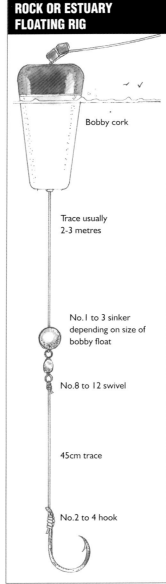

ROCK OR ESTUARY FLOATING RIG

Bobby cork

Trace usually 2-3 metres

No.1 to 3 sinker depending on size of bobby float

No.8 to 12 swivel

45cm trace

No.2 to 4 hook

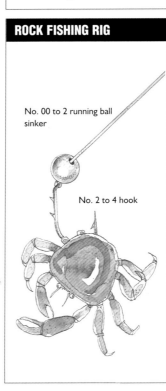

ROCK FISHING RIG

No. 00 to 2 running ball sinker

No. 2 to 4 hook

more often used for mulloway, snapper and off the ocean rocks for luderick and drummer etc.

CATCHING AND HANDLING

Low tide is when you should be out collecting these baits. At low tide, rock pools, rock walls and mangrove roots are exposed and this allows easier bait collecting. Live crabs can be bought at bait supply outlets in fishing regions, but it's usually just as easy to catch what you will use in a fishing session yourself. Only collect what you need, don't over harvest as these creatures can be decimated by indiscriminate overharvesting. Most crab baits are caught by hand and kept in a bucket with wet seaweed to keep them fresh and cool. Larger crabs may require a baited line and a spear of some sort to bring them in. Always be aware that all crabs will give you at least a minor nip if given half a chance, and the bigger models can do far worse.

STORAGE

Do not store in the sun or warm temperatures, as with most live bait, storing in cool areas will prolong the life of the bait.

If you're storing live crabs in a baitwell then ensure the water is being recirculated and aerated. Crabs are fantastic climbers so it pays to have a lid on any storage system you use for these baits.

RIGGING

One of the real benefits of using crabs for bait is that they are tough and stay on the hook longer than flimsy soft baits. Crabs should be rigged depending on their size of the bait and the size of the fish you are targeting.

Large crabs can be cut in half if they are too big for the intended fish species, or you want the baits to go further.

CRAB, RED ROCK

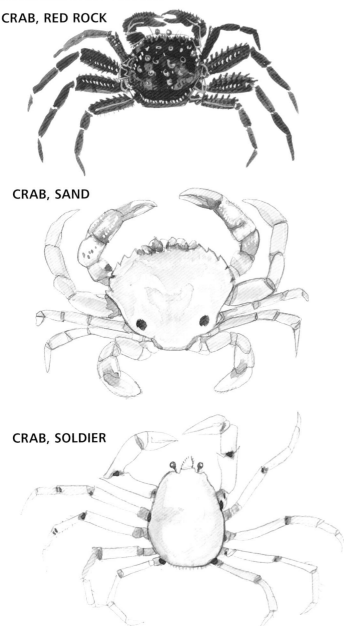

CRAB, SAND

CRAB, SOLDIER

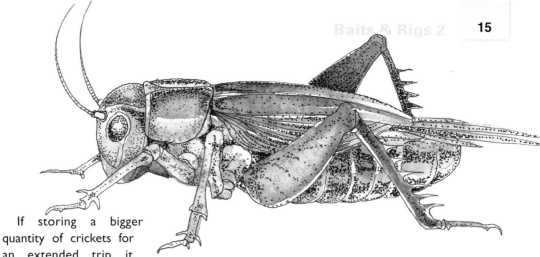

CRICKETS

As summer progresses in the southern trout states, and the heat of the day dissipates with the cooling Autumn temperatures, crickets come into their own as the number one, after dark big trout baits on our streams. They are also top baits for Australian bass and estuary perch. Unlike grasshoppers, to which these baits are related, crickets burrow underground and are most active during the night at which time they take to the wing. During the day, crickets will hold up under cover of logs, old corrugated iron, or in cracks in the dry earth waiting for night to arrive before moving about.

In season, crickets make one of the most effective after dark surface baits for big river trout.

COLLECTING

Crickets love hiding under logs and fallen timber, old pieces of tin and garden rubbish piles, dry cow pats, and virtually anywhere that it is dry and cool and out of the sun. At night, they will congregate around areas of light such as streetlights, tennis courts, sporting ovals and other areas where there is strong night lighting.

Crickets are easily collected by hand during the day or night, although you're never likely to catch big numbers in any one place, so spending some time collecting a good quantity before heading out fishing makes more sense than hoping to collect enough at your fishing location.

STORING

Crickets are best stored in a container with a secure lid and air holes. Crushed paper or grass should be placed in the container to both feed and give the insects places to hide from other crickets because they will predate on each other if left in an open area container.

If storing a bigger quantity of crickets for an extended trip, it pays to use a Styrofoam container with moist grass and crushed newspaper. Allow air for the insects, and store in a cool place. Then at the start of a new days fishing, transfer enough insects for your fishing session into a smaller container. As with all live baits, a key to prolonging their longevity is making sure they are kept out of direct heat and cool.

RIGGING

Crickets can be rigged and fished in the same way as grasshoppers. That is live on the surface and cricking to attract the fish, alive but subsurface, free drifting or below a float, or on the bottom below a running sinker. The last option is always the least successful method and rarely produces the numbers of fish that can be caught by utilising active live baits.

Crickets are a more successful general bait for lakes and all rivers than hoppers seem to be. The will consistently catch fish in lakes when fished on the surface at night or under a bubble float throughout the day. They are a very productive surface or subsurface bait for Australian bass.

When hooking crickets, it helps to leave the insects wings free to flutter about when fishing on the surface, but for fishing the baits subsurface, removing the wings will help the insect sink more readily.

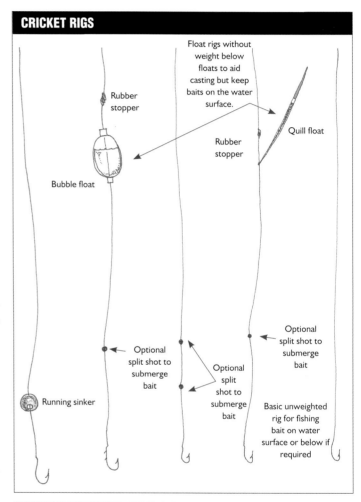

CRICKET RIGS

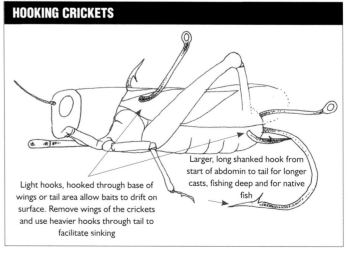

HOOKING CRICKETS

Light hooks, hooked through base of wings or tail area allow baits to drift on surface. Remove wings of the crickets and use heavier hooks through tail to facilitate sinking

Larger, long shanked hook from start of abdomin to tail for longer casts, fishing deep and for native fish

CUNJEVOI

Cunjevoi, or cunje as it is more commonly known, is regarded as one of the best, all-round baits when rockfishing for forage fish such as luderick (occasionally), drummer, bream, sweep, leatherjackets, wrasse and groper, silver trevally and tarwhine.

It is a natural bait within the tidal surge zones, so any fish species that feeds throughout those areas are likely to feed upon this bait. Its range covers from Southern Queensland to around Geelong in southern Victoria.

LOCATING

Cunje is a type of sea squirt that grows in colonies between the high and low tide marks on sloping ocean rocks and shelves, pilings and buoys in harbours and deeper estuaries. Often in areas where there is a moderate to strong wave surge zone. It can grow singularly but it is often found in larger clumps.

CATCHING AND HANDLING

Cunje is usually collected at low tide along sloping rocks that are normally under water at high tide. Collecting any bait along areas that are potentially hazardous due to wave action should be done with extreme care, and this is especially the case with cunje as the best bait is often closer to where there is wave surge.

A short and strong bladed knife is used to cut through the leathery casing to expose the

CUNJEVOI

red meat inside. This meat is then extracted and placed in a bait bucket or carry pouch for use after collecting the required amount for your immediate fishing needs.

STORAGE

Cunje flesh can be stored for later use by placing in a plastic storage container and lightly salting before storing in your freezer.

Please note there may be regulations regards how much cunje bait you can collect at any time. It is your responsibility to make yourself aware of current regulations in this regard.

RIGGING

The key to rigging cunje is to make sure that the hook goes through the firm part of the bait to keep it on the hook when casting and to avoid it be removed by picker fish. The hook size you use will be determined by the size of

Where found: Is found between the low and high tide marks on the edge of low reef areas, sloping rocks, boulders, channel markers, buoys and in rock pools.

Gather or catch it: You will need to use a robust short bladed knife to cut through the leather exterior of the cunjevoi to expose the red meat inside.

Storing: Once taken out of the outer casing you can either use the meat straight away or place it in a plastic container, lightly salt it and store in your freezer for later use. Make sure that you put the date on the lid to ensure you use the freshest container each time you go out.

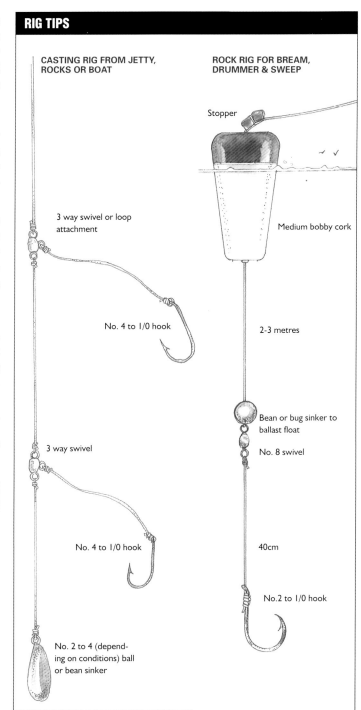

RIG TIPS

CASTING RIG FROM JETTY, ROCKS OR BOAT

3 way swivel or loop attachment

No. 4 to 1/0 hook

3 way swivel

No. 4 to 1/0 hook

No. 2 to 4 (depending on conditions) ball or bean sinker

ROCK RIG FOR BREAM, DRUMMER & SWEEP

Stopper

Medium bobby cork

2-3 metres

Bean or bug sinker to ballast float

No. 8 swivel

40cm

No.2 to 1/0 hook

Main line or leader

Breathing holes

Whole cunjevoi

Hook to suit targeted fish species

Half a piece of cunjevoi

the bait you're using and the fish you're targeting. Suicide hooks are ideal for these baits because of their curvature, and sizes from #2 through to 3/0 cover most bases.

Large cunje can be cut up into several pieces, but make sure you leave some soft fleshy part on each cut bait. Don't be afraid to use quite large baits because the fish species that regularly feed on cunje are used to harvesting big cunje as well as small.

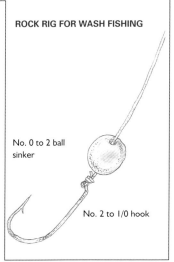

ROCK RIG FOR WASH FISHING

No. 0 to 2 ball sinker

No. 2 to 1/0 hook

CUT BAITS

There would be very few saltwater anglers that haven't used some type of cut bait during their fishing career. If you're after a feed of fish. Learning how and what cut baits to use is a basic skill that can be used for any number of target species and using numerous types of cut bait.

BEST BAITS

Some of the best cut baits come from fish species that have oily and coloured flesh, species such as slimy mackerel, bonito, yellowtail, herring and small tuna all make excellent cut bait.

Of course, using cut baits is more about just cutting up pieces of the preferred bait fish and threading it on a hook. What size of bait to use, what shape, what species and how to present it to the fish is often critically important to getting the best from your bait.

FRESH IS BEST

Once cut baits are old, dry and flaky their appeal to any target fish diminishes considerably. Firm, oily and well coloured cut baits that will stay on the hook and not be easily got off the hook by unwanted picker fish is just as important as the rig you use. Fresh bait will stay attached when rigged correctly and release its aroma and oils to draw target fish to its location.

HOW TO PREPARE BAITS

Cutting baits with some skin attached helps to keep the bait attached, and this goes for longer strip baits or smaller cube baits. Filleting fish as you would for eating is the way to go, as this will give you the flesh still attached to skin, and after any attached loose flesh etc is trimmed, these whole fillets can even be used at times depending on the size of the baitfish and targeted fish. Often bigger species such as kingfish, snapper, mulloway and sharks will happily take a whole fillet of yellowtail, mackerel or mullet in fact.

A sharp knife is a necessity when filleting and cutting down strip and cubed baits, it's important with strip baits particularly, to cut the strips clean and thin, and keep them streamlined so that the present well and don't roll around, but wave enticing when retrieved on hanging in the current.

Strip baits should range in size depending on the target species, bream etc will happily hit baits about the length of your little finger, while hungry flathead and snapper will easily devour a strip bait twice that size when drift fishing.

Cubes of cut bait are more often used when berleying and cubing for tuna

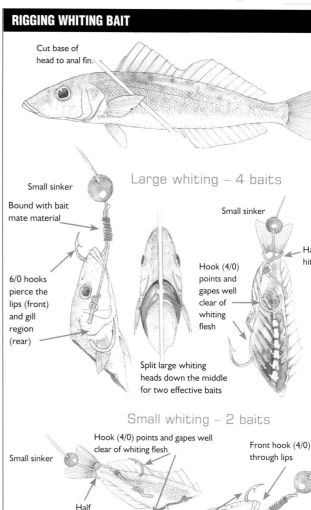

RIGGING WHITING BAIT

Cut base of head to anal fin.

Large whiting – 4 baits

Small sinker

Bound with bait mate material

6/0 hooks pierce the lips (front) and gill region (rear)

Small sinker

Half hitch

Hook (4/0) points and gapes well clear of whiting flesh

Split large whiting heads down the middle for two effective baits

Small whiting – 2 baits

Hook (4/0) points and gapes well clear of whiting flesh

Small sinker

Front hook (4/0) through lips

Half hitch

Hook points well exposed

Bound with bait mate material

Rear hook (6/0) through gill region

Fillet one side of the tail section making two baits

Small sinker

Half hitch

Bound with bait mate material

Hook (4/0) points well exposed

and sharks, or when using small fingernail sized cubes on small hooks to catch live bait.

RIGGING

Again, the method used to rig cut baits to hooks varies greatly depending on the size of the bait and the targeted species. Ganged rigs are popular when chasing fish such as tailor, sharks, wahoo etc that have sharp teeth, while a single hook at the broad end of strip bait allows for a very attractive and enticing swimming bait. Other times a large hook is threaded through the cut bait to present the bait as a stationary bait.

It's important to think about how the bait will hold to the hook during and after the cast, often using a half hitch of line

or a single hook at the head of the strip bait will prevent the bait folding up on itself at the bottom of the hook. A waving, natural and well-presented strip bait will often out fish 'lumps' of cut bait on a hook when targeting fish such as snapper, kingfish, large flathead and bream, and mulloway.

Larger cut baits are excellent for chasing mulloway in the surf.

CUTTLEFISH

uttlefish are related to squid and octopus, and are used as bait for the same species as the other two mentioned. And just like the other two mentioned, they can be both bait and food for anglers, although cuttlefish do tend to be a quite a bit tougher than both squid and octopus.

Never the less, the fish don't tend to mind their toughness of flesh, and all the fish species, such as snapper, kingfish, mulloway, cobia, morwong, Samson fish and various cod will eat a well-presented cuttlefish bait.

The most common species found in southern Australian waters is one of the world's largest, and can reach weights of 5 kilograms and 60cm main body length.
They range between Ningaloo in Western Australia, southern waters including areas around Tasmania, and north to Port Jackson in NSW.

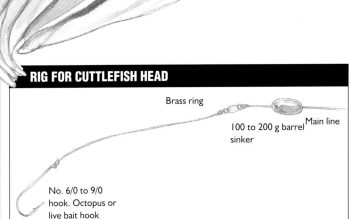

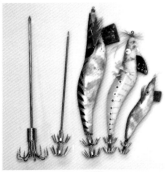

Selection of squid jigs

LOCATING AND CATCHING

Large, deep bays and harbours, along ocean rocks and out to sea are all areas where cuttlefish can be found. Most cuttlefish are incidental by catch when anglers are fishing reef areas or along ocean rocks.

For the most part they aren't targeted for bait as their capture cannot be relied upon for continual bait supply.

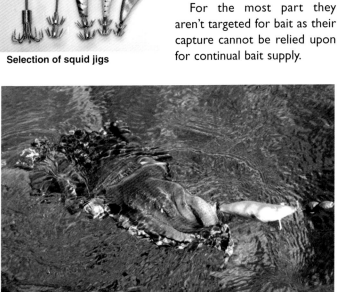

Cuttlefish caught on a jig

RIG FOR CUTTLEFISH HEAD

Brass ring

100 to 200 g barrel sinker

Main line

No. 6/0 to 9/0 hook. Octopus or live bait hook

OFFSHORE DRIFTING RIG FOR STRIP BAITS

Main line

Dropper loop 30cm

50cm

No. 3/0 Aki or Octopus hook

50cm

Dropper loop 30cm

250 to 500 g snapper sinker

No. 3/0 Aki or Octopus hook

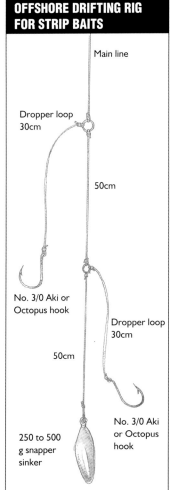

HANDLING AND STORAGE

Purchased cuttlefish can be washed and frozen for future trips, but they are a messy bait to prepare and get the useful body meat from.

RIGGING

Cuttlefish are like squid in that the head section can be used as a full bait, as can the tail and long tentacles. More often though, the cuttlefish is cut open, the gut and cuttlebone removed, and then the flesh cut into finger sized strips and used on single or ganged hook rigs as you would with squid.

RIG FOR CUTTLEFISH, STRIP OR LONG TENTACLE

Bug sinker crimped to line

Linked No. 2/0 to 4/0 hook

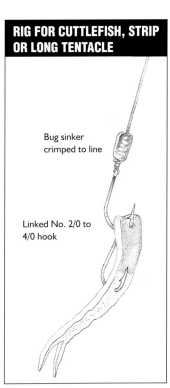

ESTUARY SHRIMP

Just like its freshwater cousin, estuary shrimp are one of the most underutilised baits when it comes to fishing for bream, estuary perch, Australian bass, whiting, flounder and other species found in estuaries and inflowing rivers.

In southern estuaries, they are a very important food source for fish, yet despite this they are often overlooked as an easily attainable and productive bait.

LOCATING

The most reliable place to catch estuary shrimp is amongst weed beds and seagrass areas. They are attractive to dead fish frames and gut, and if weed beds are located close to boat ramp and fish cleaning areas, these spots are likely to yield a good supply of bait.

CATCHING

Dragging a large, fine meshed prawn net through likely weed areas usually rewards with good numbers of shrimp if they are there. Drag the net along the bottom and through the weed to dislodge the shrimp. Always use any current in your favour by dragging into the current so the dislodged shrimp are push and held to the back of the net.

Fine meshed shrimp traps baited with a piece of fish flesh and left to sit amongst the weeds or around jetties overnight will usually give enough baits for a fishing session.

When collecting shrimp, try and only keep the larger specimens and only what you need for a fishing session. This will ensure there is always a fresh supply of shrimp to catch next time.

HANDLING

A Styrofoam esky with fresh seawater where you collected the bait, and a clump of weed will keep the shrimp in good condition during a sessions

fishing, keep in a shaded area to avoid the shrimp dying, and remove any dead shrimp mixed in with the live ones. An aerated bait bucket is also useful to keep the water fresh. Changing the water regularly and keeping the bait out of the sun is the best insurance against the baits dying.

RIGGING

Shrimp are small; so light, sharp hooks work best to present the bait as naturally as possible. Size 6 or 8 chemically sharpened hooks are usually a perfect size, and should be hooked like prawns, that is for the hook to go in at the tail and out close to on the underside of the body where the body joins the tail.

Like freshwater shrimps, these baits can be hooked two at a time, back to back on a hook, and this double bait setup means that the two baits kick against each other and this movement is very attractive to any nearby fish. The key to fishing these light baits is to use light tackle and finesse techniques to get the best from them.

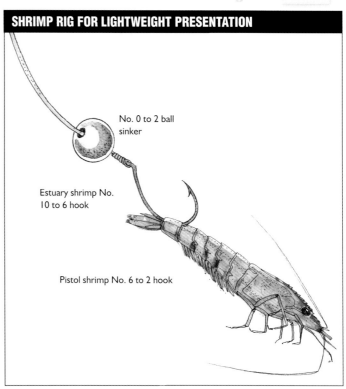

SHRIMP RIG FOR LIGHTWEIGHT PRESENTATION

No. 0 to 2 ball sinker

Estuary shrimp No. 10 to 6 hook

Pistol shrimp No. 6 to 2 hook

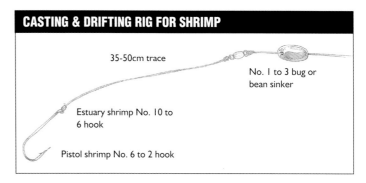

CASTING & DRIFTING RIG FOR SHRIMP

35-50cm trace

No. 1 to 3 bug or bean sinker

Estuary shrimp No. 10 to 6 hook

Pistol shrimp No. 6 to 2 hook

Yellowfin bream love nothing better than a feed of fresh estuary shrimp.

FRESHWATER SHRIMP

It's probably fair to say that wherever European carp are in great numbers, especially in lakes and slow flowing rivers, freshwater shrimp have taken a fair old 'hiding' from these noxious fish. But wherever these prawn like creatures exist in numbers, they make ideal bait for native fish and trout alike. For some species, such as Estuary perch, they are probably the number one bait in fact!

For some reason anglers fishing for native fish such as Bass, Eps, yellowbelly and silver perch seem to use these baits far more often than trout anglers do. And yet trout feeding over and along weedy or flooded lake margins are suckers for these somewhat fragile and lightweight baits. Often is the case they get used more by anglers fishing out of boats for natives as opposed to trout anglers casting from the shore. And yet, it's along the edges of rivers and lakes where these top baits, and trout exist, so next time you go out, consider taking a bait trap or drag net and getting some of the best fresh bait you can use.

Shrimp bait

LOCATING AND COLLECTING

The best place to collect freshwater shrimp is along the edges of slow flowing rivers and lakes amongst drown twigs and brush, heavy instream vegetation and throughout weedbeds. Legal, collapsible shrimp nets baited with some meat and sunken in or beside weedbeds etc. will give you a constant supply of fresh baits as required during your fishing session. Dragging a fine net through nearby weedbeds is an alternative to a shrimp trap, but they aren't as effective where there isn't a handy weedbed to drag.

STORING

Freshwater shrimp drop down the ranks from one of the best baits for many species to almost useless once they are

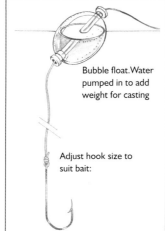

FRESHWATER LIVE BAIT RIG

Bubble float. Water pumped in to add weight for casting

Adjust hook size to suit bait:

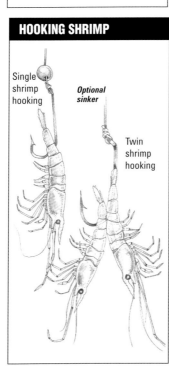

HOOKING SHRIMP

Single shrimp hooking

Optional sinker

Twin shrimp hooking

dead, fish prefer these baits kicking and flicking to be attractive, and in a lifeless state it's almost a waste of time using them. They can be stored in water from where they are caught and kept in the shade, or in a cool aerated container. But by far the best thing is to use them as you catch them, leave your trap in the water and as you need to rebait simply pull in your trap and get fresh baits. Of course, this is only possible if you're bank fishing. When fishing from a boat you will need to collect, and store your shrimp baits beforehand. Keep them cool and shaded in either an aerated live well or in a foam esky with some weed and water.

RIGGING

If ones good, two are better, and that's especially so with live shrimp on hooks. When baited two up (or three) on a single hook these baits attract fish like no other, especially so bass and EPs in rivers when fished under

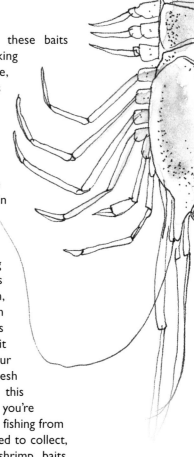

thin quill float near snags and bankside cover.

Big shrimp can be fished one to a hook, but most anglers find that with the use of two smaller shrimp per hook, clicking and flicking against each other in an attractive way, their catch rate will increase.

The key to fishing shrimps is to fish as light as possible and with finesse, they are fragile

SHRIMP RIGS

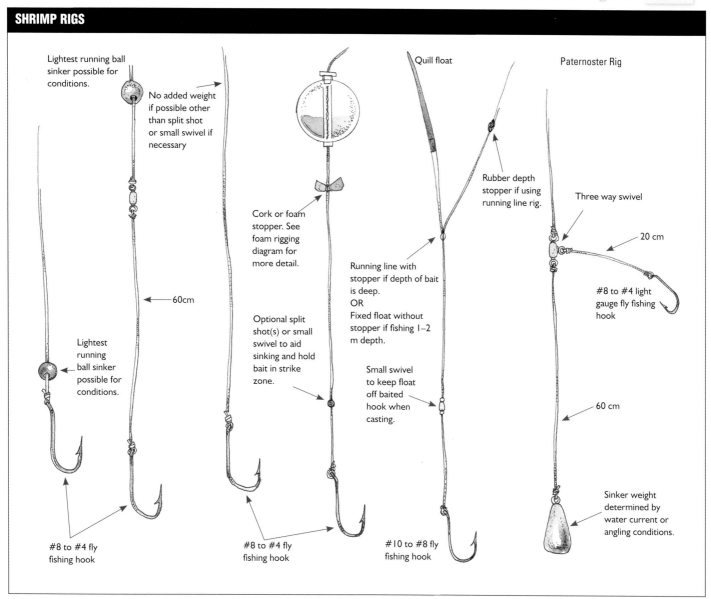

Lightest running ball sinker possible for conditions.

No added weight if possible other than split shot or small swivel if necessary

← 60cm

Lightest running ball sinker possible for conditions.

#8 to #4 fly fishing hook

Cork or foam stopper. See foam rigging diagram for more detail.

Optional split shot(s) or small swivel to aid sinking and hold bait in strike zone.

#8 to #4 fly fishing hook

Quill float

Running line with stopper if depth of bait is deep.
OR
Fixed float without stopper if fishing 1–2 m depth.

Small swivel to keep float off baited hook when casting.

#10 to #8 fly fishing hook

Rubber depth stopper if using running line rig.

Paternoster Rig

Three way swivel

20 cm

#8 to #4 light gauge fly fishing hook

60 cm

Sinker weight determined by water current or angling conditions.

baits and light in weight, small hooks with as little weight (or none) on the line will also increase your catch rate.

For trout, the best fishing using shrimp is to fish them quietly close to shore around flooded margins or flats where weedbeds are present. Flicking out the baited hook perhaps 7 metres from shore in these areas without any additional weight or at most a small split shot will often result in nice fish especially early in the season. It's crucial with this fishing often very shallow water, to stay quiet and not walk around on the bank more than necessary, and to keep the rod horizontal and the bail arm on your reel open. This will allow

the trout to pick up the bait and swim off with it before you hook up.

Bass and EPs are often best fished with a couple of live shrimp on a hook drifted near structure under a light quill float. Locating a school of fish and then a casting the float and bait upstream and allowing the bait to drift down into the strike zone. Light quill floats can also be cast directly into likely locations as well, as a slight splash of the float and bait arriving will often stir these fish species into action.

When fishing around vertical structure for redfin and yellowbelly, a paternoster rig on a tighter line is a good option. This rig can be fished stationary

or jigged (gently) vertically next to drowned trees etc. at the desired level that the schools of fish are holding.

In lakes with solid weed growth, such as Lake Wendouree and Lake Fyans in Victoria, drift fishing with shrimp under a float can be very productive as you will always be in relatively shallow weedy water everywhere, and the fish spread out right across those lakes as opposed to deep water dams. Lake Toolondo has a similar topography as the above two also.

Fishing with the smallest, lightest and sharpest hooks available in relation to the size of the shrimp you're fishing is the way to go, the lighter

the hooks, the more these small baits kick around and the longer they will live. Two or three hooked lightly through the tail will allow these baits to stay alive and active longer. If the bait dies on the hook, throw them out as berley and replace with fresh, live baits.

Small hooks will necessitate you fight a hooked fish with more delicacy, but you should also be using light line, so that will be a given.

Next time you go out with bait to fish for trout, think about trying to catch some shrimp and give them a swim. You might be pleasantly surprised.

FRESHWATER YABBIES

Freshwater yabbies (Cherax Destructor) are one of the main trout and native freshwater fish baits in Australia. Easily caught or cheap to purchase in popular recreational fishing areas, they are prime baits for redfin, yellowbelly and Murray cod. In smaller sizes and in waters where yabby populations are large, they can be big trout (usually brown trout) bait also. In many of our large impoundments, yabbies are a major diet of trout in fact.

LOCATING AND COLLECTING

Yabbies are common in freshwater rivers and dams throughout the inland areas of Victoria and NSW and are often found in big numbers by the bait collector and people looking to catch them for a feed as well. During winter, yabbies hibernate, and at that time of the year they can be hard to collect, but this isn't an issue as most fishing using these baits is during the summer months when the waters are warmer and the yabbies are in abundance. Farm dams and irrigation channels away from the main rivers often produce the best numbers of baits. The use of a drag net, or baited (with meat) drop net are the best methods for collecting good numbers of baits in a short time.

HANDLING AND STORAGE

The main requirement for keeping yabbies is to keep their gills moist and not to allow the storage container they are kept in to get hot. A Styrofoam vegetable container with a lid that can be got

from supermarkets is idea. The bottom of these should be lined with crumpled hessian and about a centimetre of water to keep and transport these baits. You will need to store the container in a shaded cool place, replace the water every few days and remove any

YABBIES

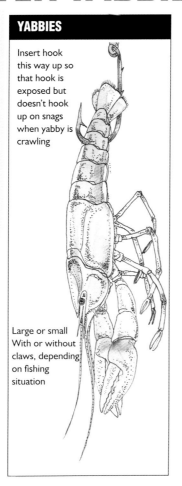

Insert hook this way up so that hook is exposed but doesn't hook up on snags when yabby is crawling

Large or small With or without claws, depending on fishing situation

BOBBING

Bobbing is performed by tying up to a submerged tree and lowering baits down to varying depths. This method is most popular with anglers chasing golden perch through late spring and over summer. As goldens will often school up and hold at a specific depth it is vital to position baits at different depths. Always position one bait right on the bottom and as the name suggests, gently lift the bait up off the bottom and then lower it back down. As you lower the bait follow the line with your rod tip until a bow forms in the line, indicating it has hit the bottom. Leave your bait there for a few minutes and then bob it up and down again.

The second bait should be positioned a few metres off the bottom. Continually adjust the depth of this bait until you are satisfied you have covered all depths in the water column. If you have marked fish at a specific depth lower your bait to this depth. Regardless of what depth you are fishing, if you feel a bite or tap, slowly lower your rod to allow the fish to take the bait.

Barbless hooks are mandatory if you intend to release fish.

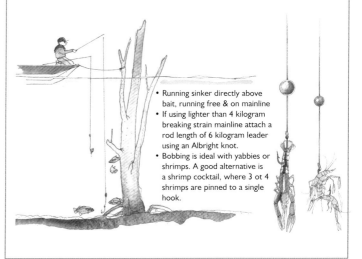

- Running sinker directly above bait, running free & on mainline
- If using lighter than 4 kilogram breaking strain mainline attach a rod length of 6 kilogram leader using an Albright knot.
- Bobbing is ideal with yabbies or shrimps. A good alternative is a shrimp cocktail, where 3 ot 4 shrimps are pinned to a single hook.

A live yabby rigged correctly, ready for the water.

WARNING

Always check regulations regarding the use of bait or drag nets before collecting bait in public waterways.

STANDARD BAIT RIGS

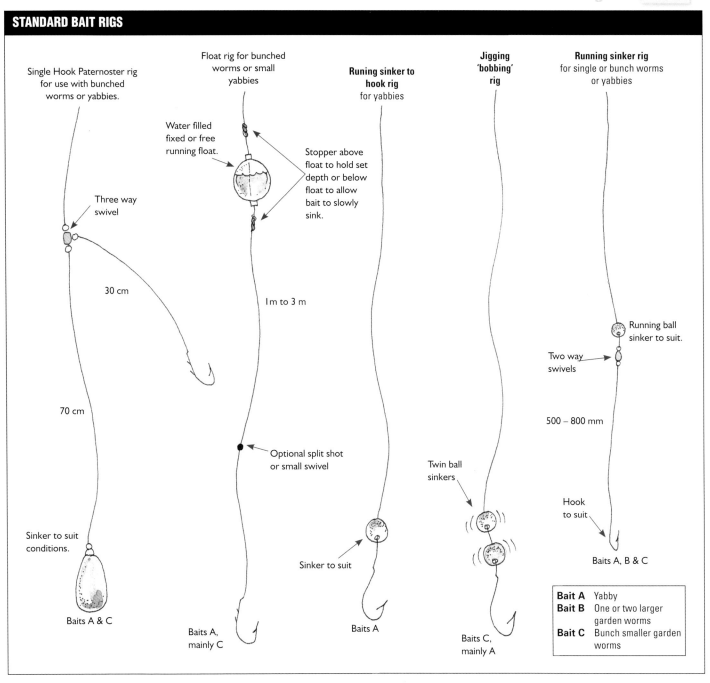

Single Hook Paternoster rig for use with bunched worms or yabbies.

Three way swivel

30 cm

70 cm

Sinker to suit conditions.

Baits A & C

Float rig for bunched worms or small yabbies

Water filled fixed or free running float.

Stopper above float to hold set depth or below float to allow bait to slowly sink.

1m to 3 m

Optional split shot or small swivel

Baits A, mainly C

Runing sinker to hook rig for yabbies

Sinker to suit

Baits A

Jigging 'bobbing' rig

Twin ball sinkers

Baits C, mainly A

Running sinker rig for single or bunch worms or yabbies

Running ball sinker to suit.

Two way swivels

500 – 800 mm

Hook to suit

Baits A, B & C

Bait A	Yabby
Bait B	One or two larger garden worms
Bait C	Bunch smaller garden worms

Freshwater yabbies are prime baits for many freshwater species including shoreline feeding brown trout.

dead yabbies to avoid the water fouling and killing others. Make sure the container lid is on as yabbies will climb up and out easily otherwise.

RIGGING

In some rivers, anglers fish dead yabbies, or section thereof that have had their shells removed so that the juices and aroma of the flesh is more pronounced to the fish. I'm of the opinion that dead whole or sections of these baits tend to attract smaller and unwanted fish such as carp. No dead baits ever outfish live baits in my view.

RIGGING BAITS

Yabbies

Thread the hook through the tail once.
Then swivel the hook around and thread it back up through the tail. The hook then sits firmly and snags less.

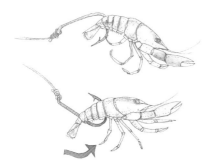

Half yabbies

To bait a tail, break off the tail and then push the hook down the underside of the tail and out.

For the head section, break the head off the yabby, crack and peel the top of the head and break the claws off.

Thread the hook through a piece of shell and pull it all the way through. Then insert the hook into a fleshy part of the yabby—ideally through a leg hole—to help set the hook well.

Shrimps

When baiting shrimps thread the hook once through the tail as with the yabby. This will hold the bait and allow it to move.

RIGS

There are a few different rigs that can be used for bobbing. The three rigs detailed here are the most common, most successful and will cover every scenario. Experiment with each of these rigs and you will find what works best for you.

When hooking up shrimps and yabbies make sure you only pin the bait once near the base of the tail with the point of the hook sitting above the crustaceans back. This will allow the bait to stay alive and flick around naturally. Please flatten the barb if you intend releasing your fish. This will help remove the hook or if the fish is hooked deeply it will greatly increase the fish's chance of dislodging the hook after release. If the fish is hooked deep and you intend to release it, don't try to extract the hook. This will not only stress the fish but has the potential to damage sensitive gills, mouth and throat. Quickly assess where the fish is hooked and if a quick, harmless removal is possible then extract the hook. If not, don't even lift the fish out of the water, simply bring it to the side of the boat, leaving it in the water and trim the line as close as possible to the hook.

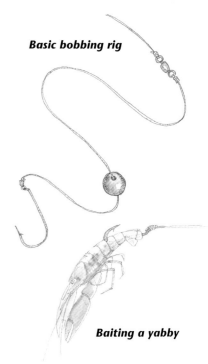

Basic bobbing rig

Baiting a yabby

Basic bobbing rig

Use a running sinker directly to the hook. Leader length should be 30–40 centimetres. Use high quality leader of 6–10 kg when targeting yellowbelly, silver perch, redfin and smaller cod. When the fish are particularly tough to hook I will go lighter in leader breaking strain. If chasing big cod or yellowbelly in very snaggy water then 8–15 kg will be required. This applies to all bobbing rigs.

When placing a hook in a yabby or shrimp I prefer to enter around half way along the inside of the tail. Push the hook all the way through so that the barb of the hook comes out the other side.

Paternoster rig

One of the most commonly used rigs is the paternoster. The sinker is fixed at the bottom of the rig with a three way swivel approximately 40–50 cm above. Attach a leader of around 30 cm to the remaining loop of the swivel as shown here. I use a locked half blood knot for all connections with this rig.

Double paternoster rig

The benefits of the double paternoster rig are that it enables the angler to experiment with two different baits on the one rig. A yabby on the lower hook and a shrimp on the upper hook are my preferred starting options. If you do not have shrimps try different sized yabbies on each hook. The other highly effective bait combination is a large, juicy scrub worm on the bottom hook and a yabby or shrimp on the upper hook. When using a worm I reduce the length of the leader so that it is less that the connecting line from the 3 way swivel to the sinker. It also pays to add a small split shot just above the hook on the lower rig. This will allow the worm to drift onto the bottom while the shrimp or yabby suspends tantalisingly half a metre above it.

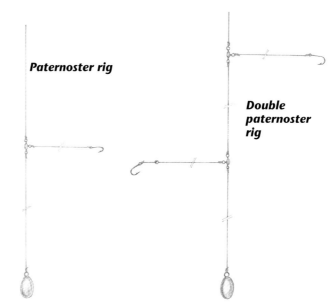

Paternoster rig

Double paternoster rig

Note that you will get the occasional tangle when using this double hooked rig however, the benefits far outweigh the odd hassle of untangling baits. To reduce tangles keep the length of leader lines to each hook relatively short at around 20 centimetres. Ensure the length of line between the two 3-way swivels and to the Arsley bomb sinker is 30–40 centimetres.

Small yabbies around 20 to 35mm in length are ideal trout and redfin bait, and can be fished on the bottom, suspended under a float or on a paternoster rig. While larger baits to around 60 mm are about as big as you should fish for trout, while larger redfin and native fish such as yellowbelly and cod will happily eat far bigger baits.

CATCHING BAIT

Crustaceans are usually active when water temperatures are warmer, catching them in winter is often a hard task in many Australian waters. As crustaceans are relatively slow moving and are often eaten by fish, this narrows down the places to find them dramatically. Slow moving waters that offer some protection are a great place to start.

Small farm dams are a great place to catch yabbies. If you are targeting them in a river then look for areas that offer protection from flow (eddies, billabongs and other backwaters) and have some structure that offers protection such as sunken timber. There are many ways to catch yabbies including scoop netting, setting traps or nets and catching them by hand using a length of string.

When catching yabbies, I collect a range of sizes because some days the fish will only eat either small or big baits—when fishing in the Darling River I found small yabbies of 5–10 cm from head to tail.

A tin of tuna, some meat and a muddy dam—a perfect scenario for yabbies.

A shrimp net baited with meat and a tin of tuna placed close to the shoreline will be productive if they are in the area.

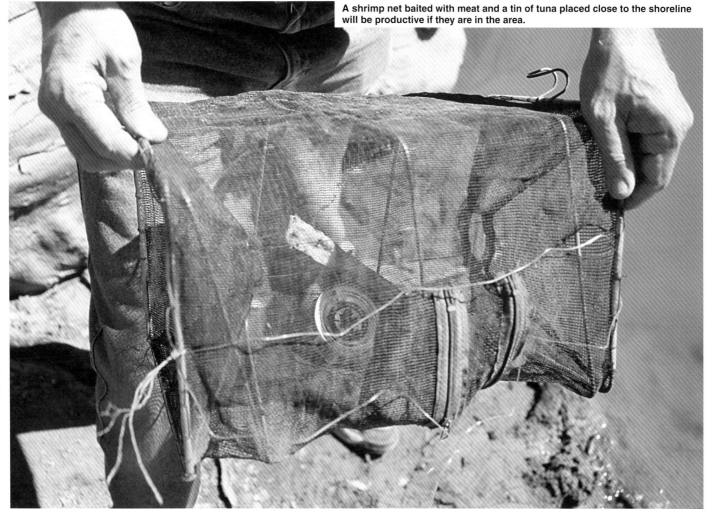

GARDEN WORMS

Common, everyday garden worms often get a bad name when it comes to their use by anglers, for some reason they aren't acknowledged as serious fish catching bait. This is a huge mistake, garden worms probably catch as many freshwater fish, if not more, than the 'prestigious' baits such as mudeyes and yabbies.

LOCATING

Garden worms love good rich soils and will often favour areas under sheets of metal, old carpet, wood or compost heaps. Anglers can cultivate areas to attract worms by composting and keeping areas in the garden moist with old hessian bags.

COLLECTING

Simply turning over soil in household garden beds will often produce enough garden worms for a day's fishing, but the best way to guarantee an ongoing solid supply of worms for extended fishing trips is by cultivating the garden bed with composted kitchen waste. Mulching garden beds and keeping the worm area shaded and moist will also guarantee supply. Worm farms are also available for sale through nurseries and garden shops, but a few months spent mulching a garden bed and creating an ongoing garden compost heap will rarely be wasted time for the garden or supply of angling bait.

HANDLING AND STORAGE

Like most fresh baits, keeping worms in a shaded/moist environment is the best way to ensure survival for an extended fishing trip. Six-pack foam eskies are good carrying containers, and all the is necessary in these is to add a layer of composting mix and friable soil with the collected worms, and this then covered with a piece of moist

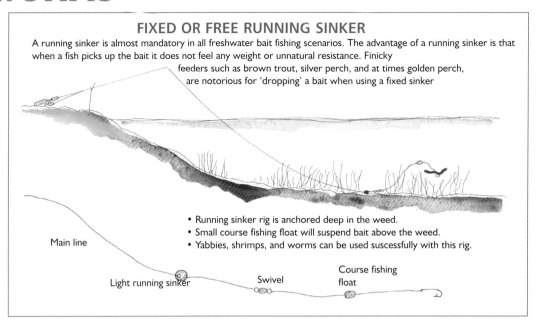

FIXED OR FREE RUNNING SINKER

A running sinker is almost mandatory in all freshwater bait fishing scenarios. The advantage of a running sinker is that when a fish picks up the bait it does not feel any weight or unnatural resistance. Finicky feeders such as brown trout, silver perch, and at times golden perch, are notorious for 'dropping' a bait when using a fixed sinker

- Running sinker rig is anchored deep in the weed.
- Small course fishing float will suspend bait above the weed.
- Yabbies, shrimps, and worms can be used sucessfully with this rig.

Main line

Light running sinker

Swivel

Course fishing float

(not dripping wet) hessian or other breathable material to create a dark, cool environment.

Never allow the soil to become 'wet' or leave the container in the sun, or get too hot, as both will quickly kill the baits.

RIGGING

The most common way of rigging garden worms involves bunching several them onto a hook. By alternating the threading of one or two worms on a hook at one time the fish are presented with an appealing wriggling bait. Always try and leave some extended tails or

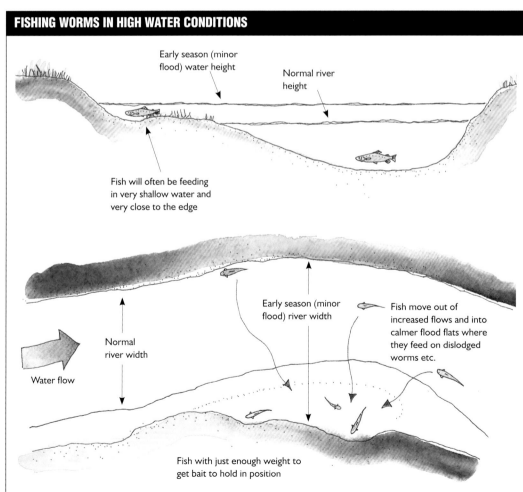

FISHING WORMS IN HIGH WATER CONDITIONS

Early season (minor flood) water height

Normal river height

Fish will often be feeding in very shallow water and very close to the edge

Normal river width

Early season (minor flood) river width

Fish move out of increased flows and into calmer flood flats where they feed on dislodged worms etc.

Water flow

Fish with just enough weight to get bait to hold in position

GARDEN WORMS

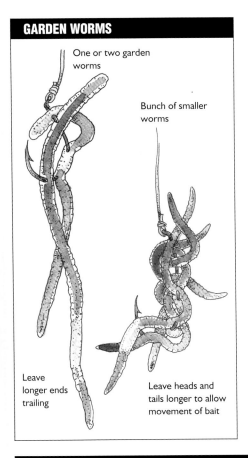

One or two garden worms

Bunch of smaller worms

Leave longer ends trailing

Leave heads and tails longer to allow movement of bait

Alex Derbogosian with one of the two Macquarie perch caught on bubble float rigs and wriggler worms.

RIGS

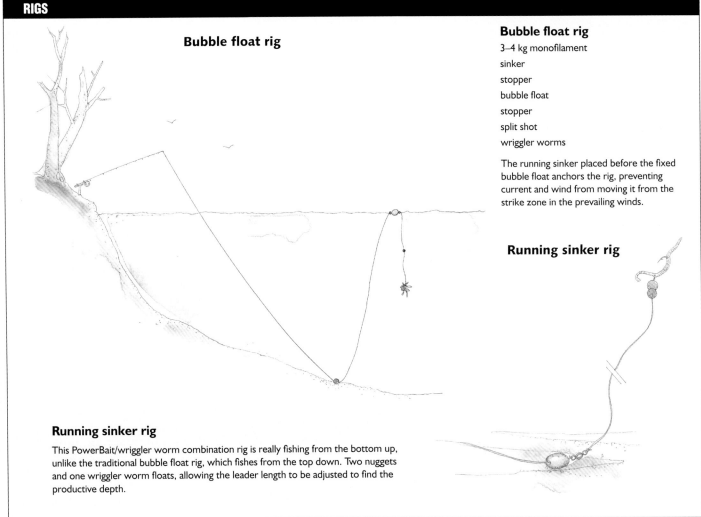

Bubble float rig

Bubble float rig

3–4 kg monofilament

sinker

stopper

bubble float

stopper

split shot

wriggler worms

The running sinker placed before the fixed bubble float anchors the rig, preventing current and wind from moving it from the strike zone in the prevailing winds.

Running sinker rig

Running sinker rig

This PowerBait/wriggler worm combination rig is really fishing from the bottom up, unlike the traditional bubble float rig, which fishes from the top down. Two nuggets and one wriggler worm floats, allowing the leader length to be adjusted to find the productive depth.

heads of the worms not pinned with the hook that can wriggle about enticingly to the fish.

Some garden worms are almost the size of small scrubworms, and when you have baits of this size it may just require the threading of one or two onto a size 6 or 8 fine wire bait hook. These larger worms are often presented singly on a hook and used for more natural presentations such as bait drifting a stream, a backwater, or bait flicking into snag areas for fish such as bass, estuary perch or structure holding yellowbelly.

While garden worms will catch fish throughout the season, they often come into their own when fishing flooded rivers or lake margins early in the season, when the waters are slightly discoloured and higher than normal. During this time of year, the rising water levels and flooded ground force the worms out of the soil and to the surface where trout are patrolling for flooded food items.

Later in the season when water levels recede and clear, these baits come into favour with anglers chasing redfin and yellowbelly.

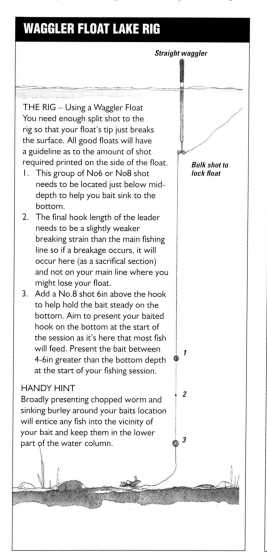

WAGGLER FLOAT LAKE RIG

Straight waggler

THE RIG – Using a Waggler Float
You need enough split shot to the rig so that your float's tip just breaks the surface. All good floats will have a guideline as to the amount of shot required printed on the side of the float.
1. This group of No6 or No8 shot needs to be located just below mid-depth to help you bait sink to the bottom.
2. The final hook length of the leader needs to be a slightly weaker breaking strain than the main fishing line so if a breakage occurs, it will occur here (as a sacrifical section) and not on your main line where you might lose your float.
3. Add a No.8 shot 6in above the hook to help hold the bait steady on the bottom. Aim to present your baited hook on the bottom at the start of the session as it's here that most fish will feed. Present the bait between 4-6in greater than the bottom depth at the start of your fishing session.

Bulk shot to lock float

HANDY HINT
Broadly presenting chopped worm and sinking burley around your baits location will entice any fish into the vicinity of your bait and keep them in the lower part of the water column.

RIGS

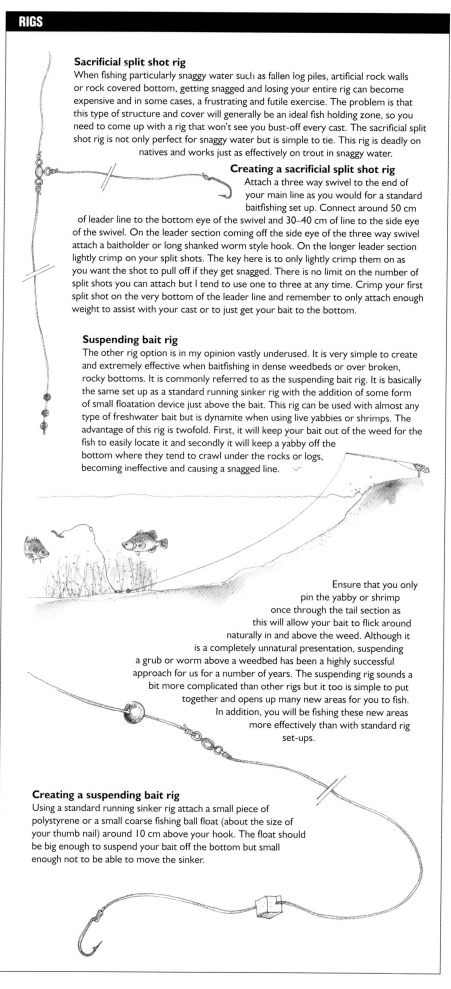

Sacrificial split shot rig
When fishing particularly snaggy water such as fallen log piles, artificial rock walls or rock covered bottom, getting snagged and losing your entire rig can become expensive and in some cases, a frustrating and futile exercise. The problem is that this type of structure and cover will generally be an ideal fish holding zone, so you need to come up with a rig that won't see you bust-off every cast. The sacrificial split shot rig is not only perfect for snaggy water but is simple to tie. This rig is deadly on natives and works just as effectively on trout in snaggy water.

Creating a sacrificial split shot rig
Attach a three way swivel to the end of your main line as you would for a standard baitfishing set up. Connect around 50 cm of leader line to the bottom eye of the swivel and 30–40 cm of line to the side eye of the swivel. On the leader section coming off the side eye of the three way swivel attach a baitholder or long shanked worm style hook. On the longer leader section lightly crimp on your split shots. The key here is to only lightly crimp them on as you want the shot to pull off if they get snagged. There is no limit on the number of split shots you can attach but I tend to use one to three at any time. Crimp your first split shot on the very bottom of the leader line and remember to only attach enough weight to assist with your cast or to just get your bait to the bottom.

Suspending bait rig
The other rig option is in my opinion vastly underused. It is very simple to create and extremely effective when baitfishing in dense weedbeds or over broken, rocky bottoms. It is commonly referred to as the suspending bait rig. It is basically the same set up as a standard running sinker rig with the addition of some form of small floatation device just above the bait. This rig can be used with almost any type of freshwater bait but is dynamite when using live yabbies or shrimps. The advantage of this rig is twofold. First, it will keep your bait out of the weed for the fish to easily locate it and secondly it will keep a yabby off the bottom where they tend to crawl under the rocks or logs, becoming ineffective and causing a snagged line.

Ensure that you only pin the yabby or shrimp once through the tail section as this will allow your bait to flick around naturally in and above the weed. Although it is a completely unnatural presentation, suspending a grub or worm above a weedbed has been a highly successful approach for us for a number of years. The suspending rig sounds a bit more complicated than other rigs but it too is simple to put together and opens up many new areas for you to fish. In addition, you will be fishing these new areas more effectively than with standard rig set-ups.

Creating a suspending bait rig
Using a standard running sinker rig attach a small piece of polystyrene or a small coarse fishing ball float (about the size of your thumb nail) around 10 cm above your hook. The float should be big enough to suspend your bait off the bottom but small enough not to be able to move the sinker.

GARFISH

For some anglers, the biggest dilemma with garfish is whether to use them as bait or to eat them. Fresh gars cooked correctly are a delight, fresh or frozen gars are also a staple bait for many species of larger fish. Garfish can be caught with hook and line or in bait traps or nets, as with all baits, fresh is best.

They are popular baits for salmon and tailor in smaller sizes, while larger gars can be used for most species such as snapper, kingfish, mackerel and even marlin.

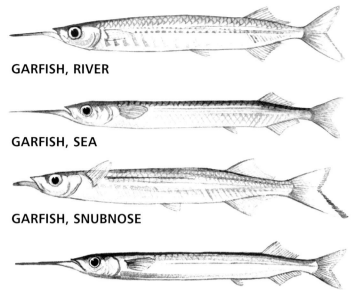

GARFISH, RIVER

GARFISH, SEA

GARFISH, SNUBNOSE

GARFISH, SOUTHERN SEA

LOCATING

Garfish predominantly feed close to the surface and most anglers would associate them around jetties, weed beds and along rock walls in estuaries. Larger sea gars, which often make better bait, can be found along ocean rocks and inlets, and on offshore bait grounds.

CATCHING AND HANDLING

If you're catching gars for fun and a feed, then light outfits using a float, small hook and bait can provide hours of entertainment. If they are feeding on the surface they also provide wonderful sport on light fly outfits. Berley is a key ingredient when targeting gars for a feed or as bait, berley will bring the gars to your position and get them feeding very enthusiastically.

Small hooks, long whippy rods and baits such as dough, bread, pieces of prawn or small pieces of fish flesh will usually produce good numbers for bait and a feed if they are brought around with berley.

In the north of Australia, gars are often taken with cast or drag nets after a school of gars are located.

STORAGE

Garfish don't like being handled, and tend to die quickly when attempting to keep them alive in bait tanks. However, live swimming baits are good, so trying to keep them alive can be worth the effort. Catching and keeping caught baits in an ice slurry will kill the gars but maintain them in a fresh condition while fishing. Gars are perfectly good bait when frozen also, and when kept initially in an ice slurry, they will be in good condition being bagged and frozen as soon as possible after the initial fishing session. Cutting off the gars bill before freezing makes for easier packing and the bill should be removed when trolling or casting these baits to avoid the trolled or retrieved bait from spinning in the water.

RIGGING

How you rig a gar bait will depend on the species of fish you're targeting. Smaller whole garfish are often rigged on ganged hooks when chasing tailor, salmon or mackerel, while a whole small gar or enticing fillet cut to size work very well on snapper, bream, trevally and flathead.

Of course, gars can also be used as cut bait when required, and pieces of gar will also catch more garfish.

Fully rigged and swimming garfish can be used to chase larger mackerel, kingfish, tuna, marlin, sailfish and other surface feeding fish, while live rigged gars are good for most species including snapper, tuna and kingfish. When live rigging it is important to use light but strong hooks so the gar can swim, and be careful not to cripple or kill the gar with the hook. Hooking through the tail or below the jaw is often the best location, while hooking along the back and above the spine is OK so long as the spine is avoided.

GARFISH (PILCHARD) RIGS

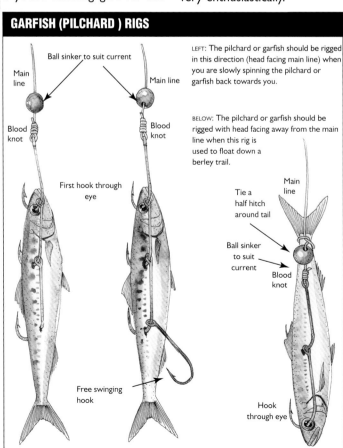

Main line

Ball sinker to suit current

Main line

Blood knot

Blood knot

First hook through eye

LEFT: The pilchard or garfish should be rigged in this direction (head facing main line) when you are slowly spinning the pilchard or garfish back towards you.

BELOW: The pilchard or garfish should be rigged with head facing away from the main line when this rig is used to float down a berley trail.

Tie a half hitch around tail

Main line

Ball sinker to suit current

Blood knot

Hook through eye

Free swinging hook

RIGS

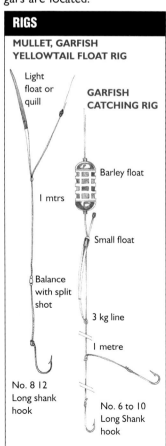

MULLET, GARFISH YELLOWTAIL FLOAT RIG

Light float or quill

GARFISH CATCHING RIG

Barley float

1 mtrs

Small float

Balance with split shot

3 kg line

1 metre

No. 8 12 Long shank hook

No. 6 to 10 Long Shank hook

GRASSHOPPERS

The onset of summer and Autumn can signal the most exciting time of the season for active bait anglers. After the Christmas holidays the weather has usually warmed sufficiently to bring grasshoppers and locusts out in numbers.

In high summer, grasshoppers offer an abundant, easily caught, rich food source for many freshwater fish, but especially so for meadow stream trout. Any stream flowing through paddocks where grasshoppers congregate in large numbers can offer superb fishing once the fish become 'keyed' in on these top baits.

COLLECTING

Strong summer winds that dry out open grassland paddocks where grasshoppers congregate, and as the grass quickly dries, often the case that the grasshoppers will migrate to feed along the still green verges of the stream you intend to fish. This is the place to not only collect them, but at the same time 'spook' a few insects into the stream to feed a few fish before you start fishing.

Grasshoppers prefer paddocks where the grass is around knee height. Farmlands that carry cattle along the borders of the river offer prime locations to collect hoppers. Paddocks that have been denuded of grass will carry hoppers, but they are far harder to catch in these areas as they tend to move about more due to lack of cover.

Grasshoppers are cold blooded and as such are extremely slow moving during the cool, dewy summer mornings before the sun gets up in the sky and warms them up enough to make them active. Catching them by hand or with a fine meshed catch net is relatively simple during the early morning. Hoppers can also be caught at night by using a bright light to attract them for collecting the night before fishing.

STORING

Collecting enough fresh live bait for the days fishing is usually easy enough without resorting to stockpiling baits. A small glass or plastic jar, with some grass added, and with the lid punctured with air holes is perfectly adequate for a day's fishing. And of course, if the baits do get low, you can generally catch a few more hoppers as you fish.

As with all fresh live bait, keeping them cool and shaded is critical to avoid them being killed with the heat.

RIGGING

Trout in streams will happily accept hoppers both on and under the surface, and selecting how you want to present the bait will have an influence on how you rig the bait regards size and placement of the hook.

For surface fishing, the use of a size 8 or 10 baitholder or fly hook, with the aid of a small bubble or quill float is all that is required to give some casting weight. Lightly hooking the hopper through the wingcase as shown will allow it to remain alive for hours, although if the fish are on, it may only last a cast or two before being eaten!

When fishing a hopper below the surface to trout or native fish, a heavier gauged hook, such as a size 6 or 8 is more appropriate to cast and get the bait under the surface and drifting about mid water or along the bottom. These sunken hoppers are often fished below a float as well to help with casting and controlling the drift. When fishing sunken hoppers, the addition of one or two split shot may be necessary to get the bait down and into the strike zone quicker.

When fishing for native fish such as yellowbelly and bass, it can be worthwhile at times to hook two or three hoppers to the hook and suspend them a metre or two below a float and fish this rig in amongst snags, standing timber or weedbeds where these fish often congregate.

The best hopper fishing for trout usually fires up around mid-morning when the hoppers start to become active, the peak activity can be around 3 or 4 in the afternoon, but once the trout are expecting hoppers and get zoned in on feeding, it is possible to use hoppers right through and into the evening.

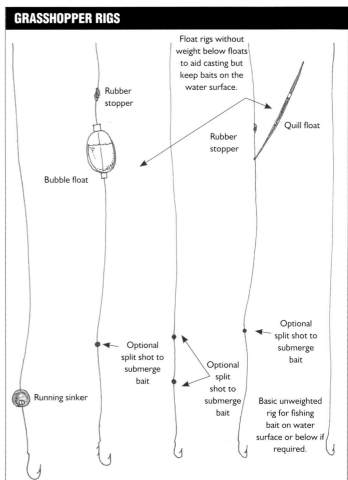

GRASSHOPPER RIGS

Rubber stopper

Bubble float

Running sinker

Optional split shot to submerge bait

Float rigs without weight below floats to aid casting but keep baits on the water surface.

Rubber stopper

Quill float

Optional split shot to submerge bait

Optional split shot to submerge bait

Basic unweighted rig for fishing bait on water surface or below if required.

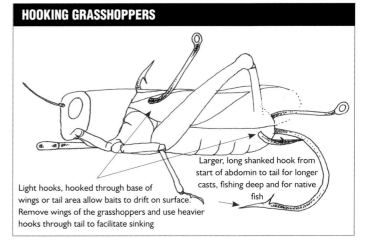

HOOKING GRASSHOPPERS

Light hooks, hooked through base of wings or tail area allow baits to drift on surface. Remove wings of the grasshoppers and use heavier hooks through tail to facilitate sinking

Larger, long shanked hook from start of abdomin to tail for longer casts, fishing deep and for native fish

HERRINGS

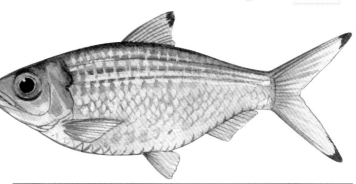

In the north of Australia, herring are an extremely important and productive bait fish. Also, referred to as shad at times, these baitfish range from Sydney to the far north and are often found in coastal rivers. They form large schools and as such offer a good opportunity for anglers to use cast nets to catch good numbers quickly.

Their range is from Central Queensland down to southern NSW and the Victorian border.

LOCATING

Tidal areas in estuaries, around jetties and tide lines, where creeks converge or in deep holes. They will be in good numbers so once you've located a few perhaps flashing their sides in the water or flicking on the surface, you are likely to encounter far more fish down deeper.

Boat anglers using sounders are often at an advantage in locating large schools of herring hanging deep in the water.

CATCHING

Unlike most other largish bait fish, herring are plankton feeders and as such are reluctant to take baited hooks, however, they can be caught using multiple bait jigs which they will hit eagerly and in good numbers when they are on. Size, 8, 10 and 12 jig hooks work well on southern herring.

In estuaries, along shelving edges and drop-offs, herring can be targeted with cast nets, especially so in Northern Queensland and Northern territory where these baits are so popular and effective.

HANDLING

Herring don't keep well in bait tanks and will perish relatively quickly, usually within a day of capture, keeper nets can work to keep some baits alive overnight at times, but catching fresh bait at the start of each fishing session is often the best bet.

The best way of ensuring live herring baits survive is to not handle them until you are ready to use them as bait.

RIGGING

Fished alive using sharp, lightweight quality hooks so as not to damage the bait. Predatory fish love live herring

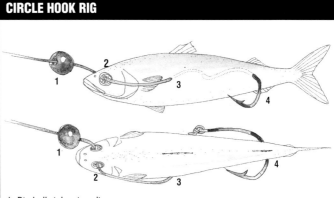

CIRCLE HOOK RIG

1. Rig ball sinker into line.
2. Thread hook through eye of pilchard and pull entire hook through.
3. Rig hook through mid point on bait and pull entire hook and line through bait on other side.
4. Rig hook point through tail region.

baits so it is important to hook them away from vital areas to allow them to swim about freely. Hooking under the bottom of the chin and up through the nose will keep the bait alive, as will hooking lightly through the upper back, away from the spine.

Herring can be free swum or fished under a float rig to keep them at a set depth.

They make a fantastic bait for most northern predatory species, both in rivers, estuaries, and around reef areas.

Strips of herring make enticing baits for bream and flathead.

Nigel Webster with a spangled emporer that fell to a small live rigged herring bait.

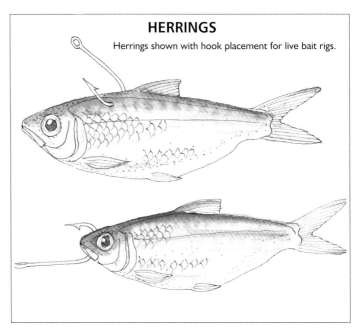

HERRINGS
Herrings shown with hook placement for live bait rigs.

MAGGOTS

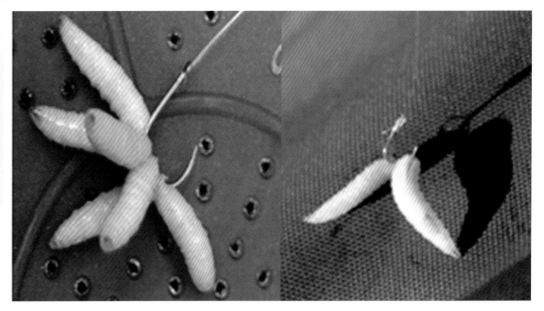

Maggots, or 'gentles' as they are often called in Europe and Great Britain are the larvae of common flies. With the advent and growth of 'coarse' fishing in Australia, the awareness of these as top baits, especially for trout, has grown considerably.

PROPAGATING

Dedicated anglers usually breed their own maggots, although there are some tackle shops that sell them commercially.

GROWING YOUR OWN AND STORAGE

Place the raw chicken breast onto a sheet of newspaper.

Place one to two inches of wheat bran into a container.

Place the newspaper, with chicken on top of it, on top of the wheat bran, but do not fold the paper over the meat.

Place the lid on the container, but do not secure it tightly. The flies need a place to enter and lay their eggs, which will become your fishing bait once they hatch. Locate the container in a quiet spot outside where it will not be disturbed by people or wildlife.

Check the chicken breast every few days for signs of fly eggs. They will look like tiny white dots, often clustered together. Continue checking on the container until you are satisfied with the amount of eggs you can see.

Wrap the newspaper loosely, but securely, around the chicken breast, to keep the maggots and their feed (the chicken breast) protected, and tightly secure the lid.

Punch tiny holes in the lid, using a safety pin. This will allow oxygen to reach the growing maggots but keep other flies and pests from entering.

Check on the container every two days until you see that the eggs have hatched and the maggots look like plump, short, white or beige worms. At this point they are ready to be used as bait.

Clean the maggots off, to prepare them for fishing, by placing them in the colander or sieve under warm running water for about one minute.

Fill the second lidded container with two inches of wheat bran.

Transfer the rinsed maggots to the second container with the wheat bran, and mix them in gently. Cover with the lid.

Store the maggots in the refrigerator until you're ready to use them for bait.

Tip

Be sure to keep the chicken breast and maggots away from children and pets to avoid illness.

Any raw meat can be substituted for the chicken breast.

Be sure to wash your hands thoroughly after handling the meat and maggots.

Discard leftover rotten meat, bran and newspaper in an outdoor trash can to avoid bringing fly larvae into your home.

WARNING

Handling raw chicken or meat can spread bacteria and viruses. Be sure to wash your hands and any tools that come into contact with the meat or the maggots very thoroughly in hot, soapy water.

RIGGING

Due to the small size of maggots, a finesse approach using small hooks and light breaking strain lines are called for. Hook sizes can vary depending on whether you are using single or multiple maggots; but generally, size #18 through to #10 fine wire fly hooks are ideal, standard weight bait hooks are too bulky for these fine baits.

To bait a hook with maggots, impale each maggot one at a time by threading the point of the hook through the maggot and slide up the hook shank. Repeat this process for each maggot you're placing on the hook. Don't overload your hook with baits, you need to make sure the hook point is exposed to achieve a hook up on the fish. Sometimes a single maggot is all that it takes to catch a fish if presented properly. Baited with their pointed head facing away from the hook, maggots tend to wiggle about and produce one of the most enticing natural fish baits available.

The two most common methods of fishing maggots are…

SWIM FEEDER RIG

These rigs rely on a constant flow of water to disperse the maggots from the berley cage setup and attract any fish back to your rigged bait.

UNDER FLOAT RIGS

Suspending maggot baits under a float allows anglers to change the depth that the bait is fished at. This depth often coincides with the depth at which fish have been sounded or attracted to via the occasional berleying using other maggots.

BERLEYING

Fishing maggots often as not relies heavily on using them for berley as well as bait, and as such, one very important thing worth noting and remembering is that using some maggots (don't overdue how many you use) as berley will increase your catch rate. By not overdoing the amount of berley you use, I mean throwing a few loose maggots into your fishing zone occasionally to attract and get the fish to your bait, not giving them a free feed.

A nice rainbow for the smoker.

DIY SWIMFEEDER

1. Take an old film canister and drill a smaller hole in the bottom just big enough to allow monofilament line through.

2. Then drill plenty of larger holes in the circumference and the lid.

3. To attach the swimfeeder to the line thread some line through the hole in the bottom and tie a weight to the end of the line. Tie on a swivel at the other end of the short line.

4. The swivel can be threaded onto the main line above another swivel. Pull the weight up against the bottom and fill it with berley, attach the lid and the feeder is ready to cast.

Alternatively you can buy a ready-made feeder, which just needs threading onto the main line above a swivel, allowing it to run freely up the line when a fish takes the bait.

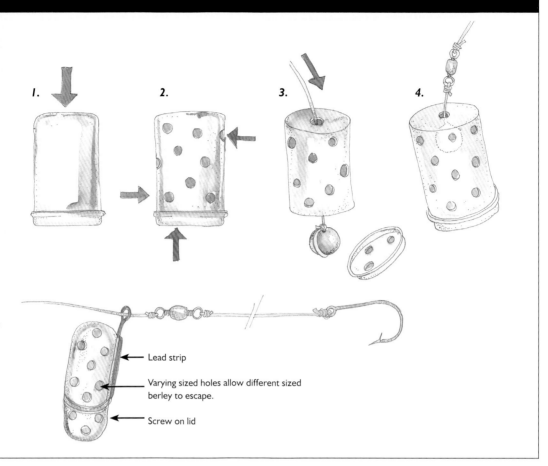

Lead strip

Varying sized holes allow different sized berley to escape.

Screw on lid

Brown trout in rivers and lakes can be successfully targeted using maggots as bait.

SWIM FEEDER RIG

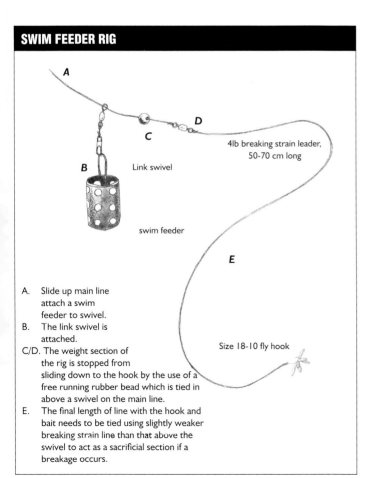

Link swivel

swim feeder

4lb breaking strain leader, 50-70 cm long

Size 18-10 fly hook

A. Slide up main line attach a swim feeder to swivel.
B. The link swivel is attached.
C/D. The weight section of the rig is stopped from sliding down to the hook by the use of a free running rubber bead which is tied in above a swivel on the main line.
E. The final length of line with the hook and bait needs to be tied using slightly weaker breaking strain line than that above the swivel to act as a sacrificial section if a breakage occurs.

MINNOWS, GALAXIDS AND SMELT

The use of freshwater baitfish is not overly common in many areas, yet when fished correctly, especially where trout and other freshwater sport fish consistently prey on smaller fish, it can be very productive bait. The most common heading of 'minnows' is used here to cover any number of small baitfish and galaxids, gudgeons, smelt, hardyheads or even small roach and redfin where these fish are in large numbers and predated upon.

Polaroiding the edges produces some exceptional browns in the winter months – this one was taken on a two hook rig.

WARNING

A word of warning, the use of live fish baits, or certain species of fish baits may be illegal in certain areas or states. Please check and abide by the regulations in the area you plan to fish before travelling with, or using live or dead fish baits.

LOCATING

Small baitfish are generally located around bankside structure such as rocks and logs, and weedbeds in shallower water where these fish head to spawn or to avoid predation from bigger fish. They can be easily located at night with the aid of a bright light or by berleying around a selected area with bread or fish food where the schools of fish are usually located.

Winter and spring are prime seasons to target trout with baitfish as they are especially active, while spring is also the season that sees whitebait migrating in Tasmania.

CATCHING AND HANDLING

Minnows are usually caught in bait traps, which can be purchased at tackle shops. These are generally funnel type traps. Long handled drag nets dragged through likely areas can also be productive. The funnel type nets rely on small baitfish being attracted to bait of some sort such as bread.

Styrofoam eskies or larger buckets (and lid) with aerators to keep the baits alive are the best option for transportation, although you might get away without an aerator if you have a large enough bucket and can regularly replenish the water from where you are fishing. Do not use tap water for this.

For best results, baitfish should always be used fresh and alive if possible. The only exception to this is if you intend to troll a minnow behind a slow-moving boat or kayak.

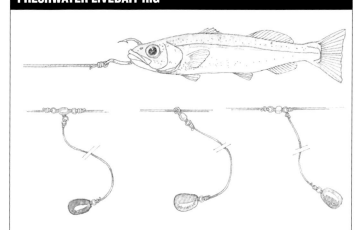
When using live baitfish, always check regularly to make sure they are still active, and if not replace with fresh bait.

RIGGING

Before anything else, you need to make sure the size of the bait you are using is suitable for the size of fish you are targeting. Freshwater sportfish are more likely to hit a live baitfish that they can consume in one hit. Smaller baits are usually preferable than large baits when it comes to live baitfish.

There are several methods that can be used for swimming a live baitfish, and most entail the use of a float of some sort. In bigger, deeper, open lakes, it is possible to 'free swim' a live bait without controlling its depth, but for the most part, using a float to hold the live bait at a set depth around weedbeds and structure is the normal rig. Another option is to use live bait under a running sinker rig and using a foam or cork float to hold the baitfish up off the bottom. A paternoster rig is also an option but these rigs can result in the baitfish

REGULATIONS

It should be noted that in some waters and States (NSW) it is illegal to use live fish as bait in inland waters. Anglers should always be aware of and obey fishing regulations.

Always catch and use live bait from the river or lake system that you intend to fish. Never translocate fish from one waterway to another and always return unused baitfish back into their natural waterway after you have finished fishing.

swimming and tangling up on the main line. Small baitfish are usually hooked through the lips when they are being trolled or being fished in any water with a current, as this positioning prevents the bait spinning. At times, it can be advantageous to rig more than one minnow to the hook, and this rigging works in a similar fashion to rigging multiple shrimp to create more movement. Baits that are hooked through the back or tail area need to be hooked lightly through the skin to avoid any injury to the spine area.

GLASSIE RIGS

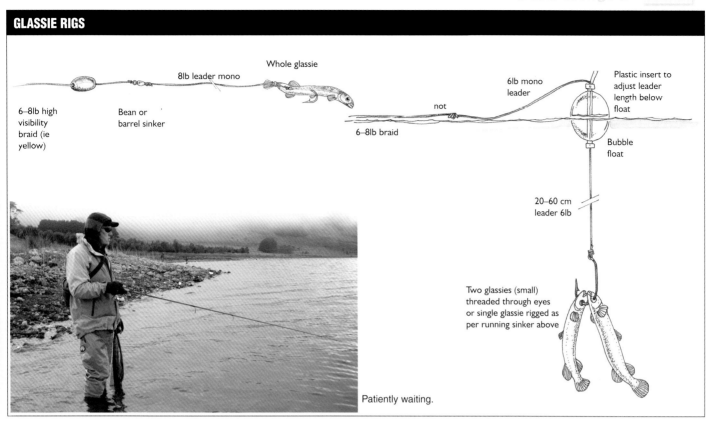

6–8lb high visibility braid (ie yellow)

Bean or barrel sinker

8lb leader mono

Whole glassie

6lb mono leader

6–8lb braid

not

Plastic insert to adjust leader length below float

Bubble float

20–60 cm leader 6lb

Two glassies (small) threaded through eyes or single glassie rigged as per running sinker above

Patiently waiting.

HOOKING BAITFISH

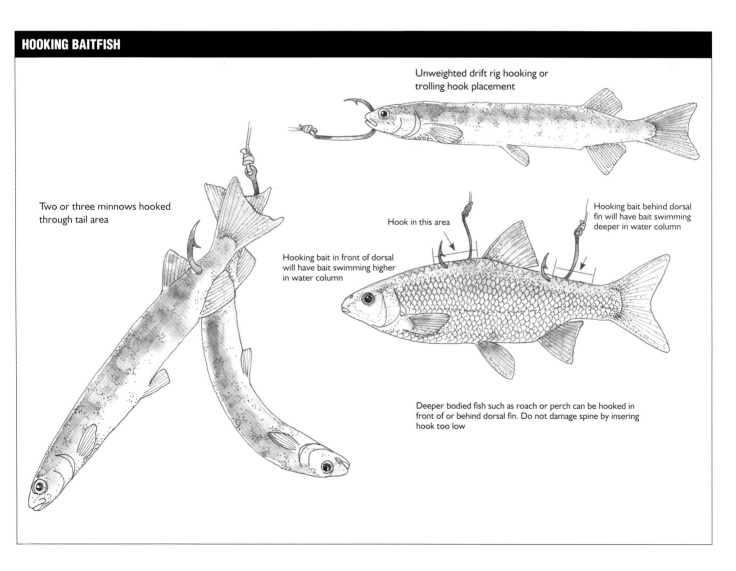

Unweighted drift rig hooking or trolling hook placement

Two or three minnows hooked through tail area

Hook in this area

Hooking bait behind dorsal fin will have bait swimming deeper in water column

Hooking bait in front of dorsal will have bait swimming higher in water column

Deeper bodied fish such as roach or perch can be hooked in front of or behind dorsal fin. Do not damage spine by insering hook too low

MUDEYES

Every serious trout angler is aware of the effectiveness and consistency of mudeye baits. They are arguably the most effective trout bait on Australian lakes no matter what the season, but especially over the warmer months of the year. Mudeyes are the nymphal stage of dragonflies.

LOCATING

Mudeyes can be found in dams, streams and impoundments; living amongst weed, on submerged timber and rocks. In the heavily weeded stillwaters it is the longer, slender species known as couta mudeye that is often most prevalent, while in streams and flowing water the is the squat, robust spider mudeye you will generally encounter living under rocks.

Both species are equally as effective as the other, although it is the couta mudeye that is usually most prevalent.

COLLECTING

Many anglers buy their mudeye baits from tackle shops to save time collecting their own. Virtually every tackle store in 'trout regions' will sell these baits. Most mudeyes are collected by dragging weedy farm dams using long handled wire nets, the weed drag up will usually have good numbers of these nymphs where these insects frequent. Large numbers of adult dragonflies around a dam or weedy waterway will usually signal good numbers of nymphs are likely present.

When dragging farm dams for mudeyes and yabbies etc.

Mudeyes are popular trout bait

Prime smaller sized rainbow trout will often feed on mudeye baits.

please ask permission from the owner before doing so.

STORAGE AND HANDLING

Mudeyes can be kept alive for long periods in a cool Styrofoam esky with a good amount of weed and water from the collection point. So, long as the water is replaced occasionally, every five days or so, and the water is kept cool and the esky in the dark, mudeyes can be kept for several weeks in these containers.

Mudeyes are quite hardy, but they are very susceptible to anything that can spoil or poison the water they are stored in. They are also susceptible to sunscreens and insect repellents on angler's hands, so handle with clean hands and fresh water to maintain them in good condition.

RIGGING

Mudeyes should be fished so

that they appear as natural as possible in the water and as such this is achieved by using small bait holder or fly fishing hooks around size #14, #12 or #10.

While some anglers fishing lakes feed a mudeye onto a long shank narrow hook from vent up through the body and out the mouth or out near the insect's head, this method is not preferred. It quickly kills the insect and detracts from its fishing effectiveness on most occasions in still water. This rigging method is often best when using mudeyes in rocky smaller streams where the current is rougher and repeated casting is involved. When fishing these waters, rigging this way will usually ensure that the bait remains on the hook longer with repeated casts.

The most reliable and successful method to fish

FLOAT RIG FOR WINDY CONDITIONS

Often the angler needs to cast out a float rig into a wind. This rig anchors the float and prevents it from being blown back to shore.

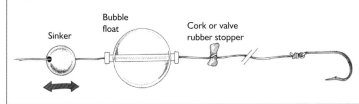

Sinker

Bubble float

Cork or valve rubber stopper

Onshore wind

Stopper

Bubble float

Bait

Sinker

The sinker separates from the float and sinks to bottom

RIGS

mudeyes under float in lakes and larger, slower rivers is to lightly clip the hook through the insect's wing case area to avoid critically damaging the insect. By carefully hooking it in this way you allow the mudeye to move about and remain lively whilst fishing.

In lakes and larger rivers mudeye are mostly fished below a float of some sort, this is usually a bubble float that can be filled with water to allow for some casting distance of these light baits. In these situations, the bait is fished at a predetermined depth (or allowed to drift slowly deeper) below the float and this depth is set using a stopper of some sort. When using this method from the bank it is important that anglers use line grease on the line above the float so that the line between rod and float doesn't sink to the bottom and get caught or snagged up.

If fishing mudeyes below a float directly beside a boat (as might be done at Dartmouth Dam amongst timber and other deeper lakes) then greasing the line isn't necessary. In these situations, the mudeye can be allowed to sink down very deeply beside the boat (with the aid of the smallest split shot or swivel a metre above the bait) before clipping on a small piece of cork or fine quill float to hold the desired depth.

Trout will usually take a mudeye lightly before swimming off with it and it is often imperative to allow the trout to do so before setting the hook. Setting the rod at a low angle and allowing slack line or fishing with an open drag is the best method to achieve unhindered line flow when the trout picks up the bait. Laying a tarp of some sort on the ground under the reel area will also give some free line an area to sit without getting caught up in grass and twigs which can hinder free flowing of line when the fish

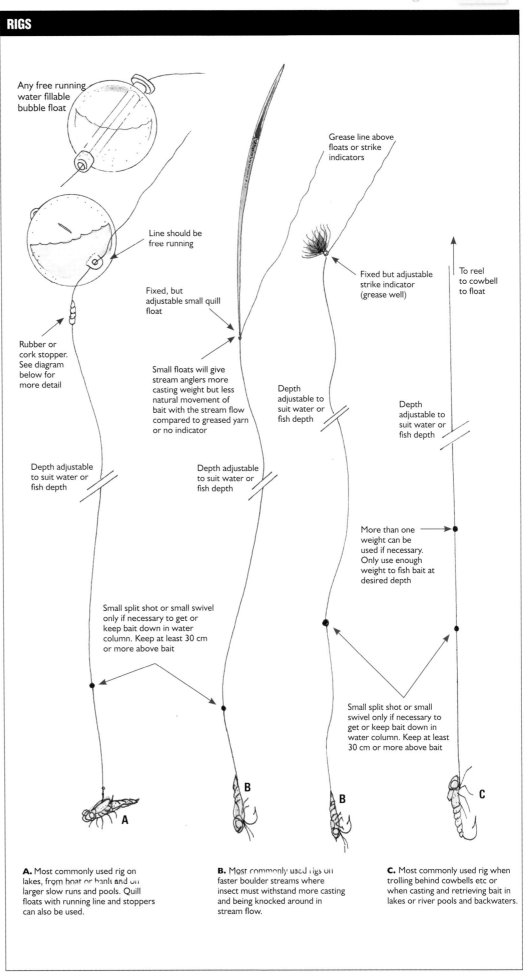

Any free running water fillable bubble float

Line should be free running

Rubber or cork stopper. See diagram below for more detail

Depth adjustable to suit water or fish depth

Small split shot or small swivel only if necessary to get or keep bait down in water column. Keep at least 30 cm or more above bait

Fixed, but adjustable small quill float

Small floats will give stream anglers more casting weight but less natural movement of bait with the stream flow compared to greased yarn or no indicator

Depth adjustable to suit water or fish depth

Grease line above floats or strike indicators

Fixed but adjustable strike indicator (grease well)

Depth adjustable to suit water or fish depth

To reel to cowbell to float

Depth adjustable to suit water or fish depth

More than one weight can be used if necessary. Only use enough weight to fish bait at desired depth

Small split shot or small swivel only if necessary to get or keep bait down in water column. Keep at least 30 cm or more above bait

A   B   B   C

A. Most commonly used rig on lakes, from boat or bank and on larger slow runs and pools. Quill floats with running line and stoppers can also be used.

B. Most commonly used rigs on faster boulder streams where insect must withstand more casting and being knocked around in stream flow.

C. Most commonly used rig when trolling behind cowbells etc or when casting and retrieving bait in lakes or river pools and backwaters.

SPIDER MUDEYE

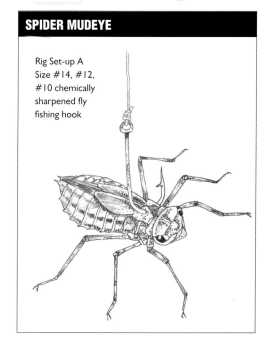

Rig Set-up A
Size #14, #12,
#10 chemically
sharpened fly
fishing hook

COUTA MUDEYE

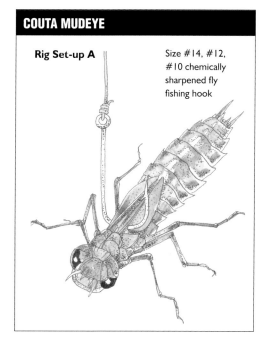

Rig Set-up A

Size #14, #12,
#10 chemically
sharpened fly
fishing hook

SPIDER OR COUTA MUDEYE

Rig Set-up B

Hook should enter or
exit at tail of insect

Size #4, #6, long shank, wide gape,
straight eye baitholder hook, depending
on length of bait

Hook should
enter or exit at
start of thorax.

Rig Set up C

Hook should enter
or exit at tail of
insect

Hook should enter
or exit at start of
thorax.

Size #4, #6, long shank,
wide gape, straight
eye baitholder hook,
depending on length of bait

BUBBLE FLOAT DEPTH ADJUSTING STOPS

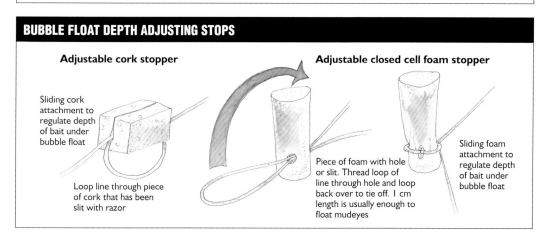

Adjustable cork stopper

Sliding cork
attachment to
regulate depth
of bait under
bubble float

Loop line through piece
of cork that has been
slit with razor

Adjustable closed cell foam stopper

Piece of foam with hole
or slit. Thread loop of
line through hole and loop
back over to tie off. 1 cm
length is usually enough to
float mudeyes

Sliding foam
attachment to
regulate depth
of bait under
bubble float

moves off. Always allow the fish to swim off and swallow the mudeye before setting the hook.

Mudeyes can also be fished effectively in smaller or overgrown streams with the aid of one or two small split shots. Greasing the line to within a metre of the bait is all that is necessary to achieve success along with the aid of a greased yarn indicator (as used by fly fishers) if necessary. Casting up into a run or through an undercut or into a snag pile is a great way of fishing areas that fly and lure fishermen simply can't reach. The angler just needs to be aware of and try and stay in contact with the bait as it floats through an area. The bait being picked up by a fish will usually be indicated by the line or yarn indicator dragging underwater, or stopping, or moving unnaturally in the stream flow. Simply lifting the rod slowly but deliberately against the direction of the line movement will be enough to hook a fish when using small chemically sharpened hooks. Small quill floats can also be employed on streams but these can be more of a hindrance at times on streams with lots of structure and in-stream debris.

The other method of fishing mudeyes (but not really baitfishing in my opinion) is by trolling a mudeye extremely slow behind a cowbell or flashing attractor setup. The setup entails impaling a mudeye through the mouth and out through the dead centre of its tail with a long shank, round bend fly hook of a size to match the bait. The attractor is attached to the line above the bait at a desired length away from the bait (usually at least a metre). This method is extremely effective in Lake Eucumbene, Dartmouth Dam and Lake Purrumbete to name just a few.

MULTI

Probably one of the most diverse fish on the planet, mullet in various makes and sizes offer great bait and are fun to catch as well. They are a very hardy fish and as such make top live bait when their size suits your targeted predatory species.

Mullet offer good sport off jetties and piers on light tackle for kids and adults and depending on the species being caught, they are also average eating.

LOCATING

Most mullet used for bait are smaller species such as poddy mullet. These are usually found in schools along shallow edges of lagoons and estuaries, over sand bars and along weedy edges. Larger sized mullet tend to frequent deeper areas around jetties, piers and wharves.

Mullet tend to feed along the surface like garfish and can be brought on the bite and held in an area with bread berley.

CATCHING

Hook and line, bait traps, cast nets and drag nets are all used to catch mullet, generally the smaller mullet caught in bait traps make great live bait for large flathead and other predatory estuary fish, while the larger mullet baits are more suited to barramundi, mulloway, mangrove jacks, cod etc.

Cast and bait nets where legal, are the quickest and easiest method to catch smaller bit sized mullet quickly, while a baited hook and line is more suited to catching larger mullet off piers and jetties, these larger fish are usually caught for fun and a feed instead of bait, although these larger sized mullets (500 gm) make excellent trolling baits or strip baits for larger sportfish such as wahoo, marlin and Spanish mackerel etc.

Mullet are very attracted to berley and bread is the

PUNCHY BARNARD RIG

This most effective bait rig was shown to Geoff Wilson by reknowned angler Glen Mitchell and is one of his favourites for mulloway. You need a small fish; anything from a large pilchard to a mullet, or perhaps a small but legal size Australian salmon. Hook size will usually be from 6/0 to 9/0 depending on the size of the fish being used for bait.

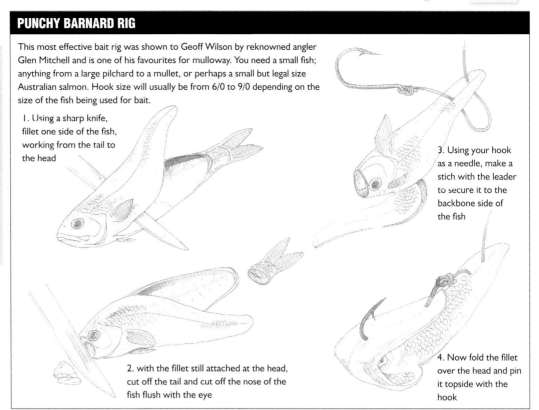

1. Using a sharp knife, fillet one side of the fish, working from the tail to the head

2. with the fillet still attached at the head, cut off the tail and cut off the nose of the fish flush with the eye

3. Using your hook as a needle, make a stich with the leader to secure it to the backbone side of the fish

4. Now fold the fillet over the head and pin it topside with the hook

SWIMMING MULLET

The gills and mouth on the mullet are sewn together to avoid damage to the bait caused by water as it is trolled. A sinker is tied on the bridle in close to the top of the head to help the bait stay in the water and even maintain a head down attitude. The hook is positioned inside the bait, which is then sewn together.

preferred berley and bait for these fish, although they will take hooks baited with sandworm or prawn as well. Dough baits are very successful because they can be moulded to fit the small hook sizes that need to be used.

HANDLING AND STORAGE

Mullet are very hardy fish and will tolerate some handling, having said that though, the less handling and stress on the bait the better if you intend to use them as live bait. They can be stored live in aerated bait tanks or buckets so long as you regularly give them changes of water.

Mullet that are caught with the intent of using as trolled baits should be as fresh as possible and therefore are best caught personally rather than bought.

RIGGING

Small mullet fished live under a float or dropped/drifted down into snags or around rock bars are top bait up north in the tropics, while live fished mullet suspended off the bottom down south are prime baits for mulloway, large flathead, salmon and tailor. Hooking live baits through the top and bottom lips is the preferred method in areas where there is any stronger current, while hooking through the upper back near the first dorsal fin is best in slight current areas or when drifting from a boat.

A double hook rig, with one hook through the lips and the trailing hook through the back offers good insurance to increase hook-up rates on bigger fish. Dead baits can be used whole when chasing

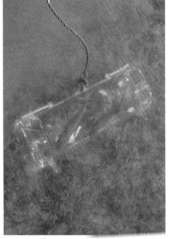

This mullet trap obviously works, with small mullet having been lured into it by the attraction of plain white bread bait.

bottom fish and sharks, while strip baits are also good and allow the angler to cut the strips to match the size of the rig being used and the fish being sought.

MUSSELS

Mussels are a top bait for any fish species that graze feed, fish such as bream, leatherjackets, morwong, whiting, parrotfish, snapper, sweep and drummer will all feed on these baits. Most common in the southern regions of Australia, and where permitted, easily collected, they are a staple bait and berley, particularly for whiting in the southern states.

LOCATING

Mussels form into large clusters and can be found on pier pilings, wharfs, bridge pilings, navigational markers, mooring lines and along foreshore rocks and rock walls.

They range from Mindarie in Western Australia, southern waters including Tasmania, and as far north as Forster in NSW.

They prefer areas of high water movement, but needs more than 15 parts per thousand (about half normal sea water) to survive.

COLLECTING

Where it is permissible to collect them, the clusters of mussels can simply be torn from their location. They are easily collected so long as you can access them (often best done at low tide) and you have good hand protection to avoid being cut by any sharp shell edges. A sturdy knife can be useful to remove whole clumps rather than a few shells at a time.

HANDLING AND STORAGE

Because these baits are often found close to the area you're likely to be fishing, they are often collected fresh at the start of the fishing session. Stored in a cool place they will survive for a period of a few days. Mussel can be stored by salting the flesh after removing from the shell and storing in jars and kept in the fridge, or placing the flesh into a lidded plastic container, covered in seawater and placed in the freezer for later use.

Mussel flesh that has been salted is just as good as fresh mussel baits and even toughens slightly due to the salting which can help keeping it on your hook.

RIGGING

Because of their soft texture, it is imperative that you do everything to keep the flesh on your hook when fishing these baits, like all soft baits, the number one best practise is to use whippy soft rods that tend to soften the cast and allow the fish to eat the bait rather than tear it off the hook.

Threading the bait onto the hook is best done by firstly threading the tougher black central are onto the hook and then also threading the softer flesh a few times after that. A half hitch of the line back over the bait also helps to secure the bait to the hook as does the minimal use of a couple of turns of bait-mate elastic if needed.

LIGHT BITES

If you are after fish that are finicky and bite lightly, consider using a solid tip rod as this type has an increased degree of sensitivity than totally hollow fibreglass rod tips. A selection of interchangeable solid tips makes one rod more suited to different applications of fishing methods. When fishing turbid water thosae baitrs that smell such as shellfish like mussels and woms will often prove the better choice.

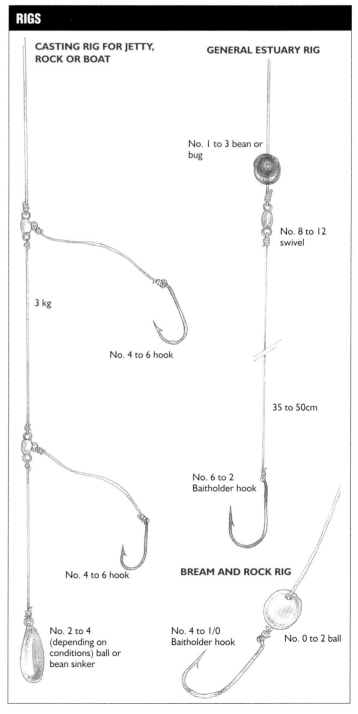

RIGS

CASTING RIG FOR JETTY, ROCK OR BOAT

3 kg

No. 4 to 6 hook

No. 4 to 6 hook

No. 2 to 4 (depending on conditions) ball or bean sinker

GENERAL ESTUARY RIG

No. 1 to 3 bean or bug

No. 8 to 12 swivel

35 to 50cm

No. 6 to 2 Baitholder hook

BREAM AND ROCK RIG

No. 4 to 1/0 Baitholder hook

No. 0 to 2 ball

OCTOPUS

Whole or cut sections of octopus are very popular baits for many offshore and estuary anglers and various fish species. The flesh is tough like squid and as such is an ideal bait for use when small picker fish are about. And just like squid, octopus is now seen as something of a table delicacy, and as such it is now very expensive to purchase for bait use.

Octopus vary greatly in size from smaller baits that are best used whole to large creatures that are best cut up to smaller, manageable baits.

LOCATING

Octopus frequent rock shelf and crevices, break walls and rock pools, and in amongst weed and kelp beds throughout intertidal zones and estuaries. Often the octopus found in these areas are large and not as popular as bait. The smaller octopus, which are more popular for bait, are more often trawled up by professional fishermen and these can be purchased directly from the pro boats or local bait shops.

CATCHING

Octopus are generally most active at night, and can be targeted with hand nets or spears using a bright spot light like flounder fishing. Areas along rocky shelves, rock pools and weed beds can all be productive areas. They can also be caught in baited traps made from PVC plumber pipe, with one end blocked off and a rope attached these tubes can be lowered into suitable areas and left overnight for any octopus to eat the bait and take up residence. These traps can be retrieved the following day and will often be occupied by and octopus if placed in reliable octopus' territory.

They can also be caught on baited squid jigs. Octopus predate on crabs, so using these as bait on the jigs or in the PVC tube, or other traps increases the likelihood of attracting an octopus.

HANDLING

Octopus are amazing escape artists, they can get through holes and slits in containers you wouldn't imagine, they are also excellent climbers, so if you intend to use them as live bait for fish such as kingfish and mulloway, make sure the container is fully secure to stop them escaping. Dead full baits or sections thereof are the most popular form of using octopus as bait. To quickly and humanely kill any octopus you can simply drop them straight into an ice slurry.

Anglers hunting for octopus should make sure they are familiar with the deadly and highly toxic blue ringed octopus and avoid them at all costs, if you come across tiny octopus that light up with electric blue bands do not handle them. Anglers also need to avoid allowing octopus to get their sharp parrot like beaks anywhere near their fingers or flesh as a nasty bite can be extremely painful.

RIGGING

Depending on the size of the bait, octopus can be used whole for larger target species such as mulloway and kingfisher, or the head removed and the tentacles used as cut bait for offshore bottom species. Strip sections and whole tentacles make good, tough baits for bottom species such as snapper and reef fish.

The real benefit of octopus is that like squid, it is very tough and stays on the hook even with small bottom picking fish about.

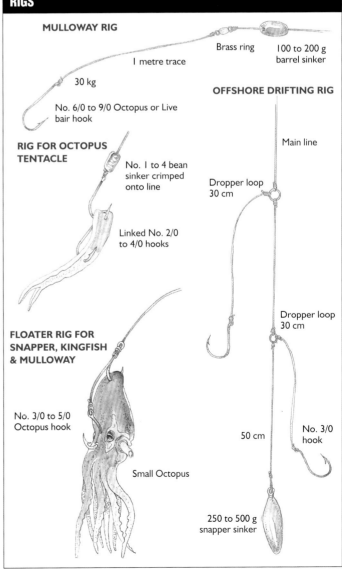

RIGS

MULLOWAY RIG

Brass ring
100 to 200 g barrel sinker
1 metre trace
30 kg
No. 6/0 to 9/0 Octopus or Live bair hook

RIG FOR OCTOPUS TENTACLE

No. 1 to 4 bean sinker crimped onto line
Linked No. 2/0 to 4/0 hooks

OFFSHORE DRIFTING RIG

Main line
Dropper loop 30 cm
Dropper loop 30 cm
50 cm
No. 3/0 hook
250 to 500 g snapper sinker

FLOATER RIG FOR SNAPPER, KINGFISH & MULLOWAY

No. 3/0 to 5/0 Octopus hook
Small Octopus

PILCHARDS

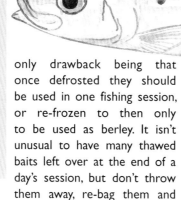

I f there is one bait that is synonymous with recreational saltwater fishing it would have to be pilchards. They are an extremely important bait for many saltwater fish species including snapper, flathead, salmon, tailor, yellowfin tuna and even chinook salmon in the carter lakes in Victoria. Their versatility as bait allows them to be used in a variety of waters including estuaries, off the rocks and surf beaches, and far offshore.

LOCATING

Pilchards are a common schooling forage fish of cooler waters, taken in large numbers for fishing bait, pet food, aquaculture food, and increasingly as food fish.

Pilchards are commercially netted in the south-western area of Australia where they are snap frozen and packaged to sell as bait in tackle shops. They are arguably the most commonly used packaged bait around Australia's southern and eastern seaboard.

CATCHING

Pilchards are only taken by commercial fishermen in purse seine, or less commonly, in beach seine nets.

While it is possible to catch your own pilchards, or similar baitfish, with nets and small baited hooks, most recreational anglers after a reliable source of these baits purchase pilchards as frozen bait in tackle shops.

HANDLING

Frozen pilchards are extremely convenient, with perhaps their

Pilchards can be mounted on 3/0 to 4/0 ganged hooks or threaded onto a single long shank 5/0 to 6/0, depending on bait size.

only drawback being that once defrosted they should be used in one fishing session, or re-frozen to then only to be used as berley. It isn't unusual to have many thawed baits left over at the end of a day's session, but don't throw them away, re-bag them and take them home. Thawed and refrozen pilchards make ideal berley, but they aren't suitable for baiting onto a hook.

Selecting quality frozen pilchards becomes easier after you've tried to use poor quality frozen baits that split, break or won't stay on a hook because of the poor flesh. Selecting bright and fresh looking frozen pilchards makes a huge difference to the enjoyment of a day's fishing.

RIGGING

The most common way of rigging pilchards for fish such as mackerel, salmon, tailor or coral trout is with a three or four hook gang hook rig. The size of the hooks used in the rig will be determined by the length of the pilchards being used. A key to rigging on ganged hook rigs is to make sure that the bait stays straight and flat, so that it will present most naturally to the target fish. If the bait is twisted or curved it will spin and twist in the water and not be as attractive.

When targeting less aggressive or smaller mouthed fish such as bream and snapper, using a double or single hook presentation with half or only the head section of the pilchard can be more practical.

When using cut sections of pilchard, the central stomach section of the bait is usually

used as berley because it is fragile and hard to retain on a hook, while the best cut sections for use with single or double hook rigs are the head or tail section.

PILCHARD (GARFISH) RIGS

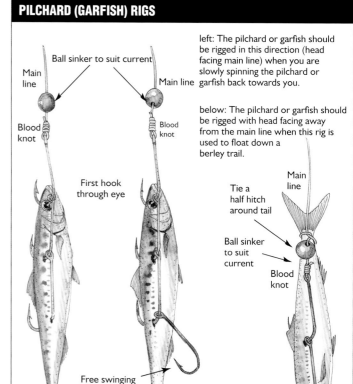

left: The pilchard or garfish should be rigged in this direction (head facing main line) when you are slowly spinning the pilchard or garfish back towards you.

below: The pilchard or garfish should be rigged with head facing away from the main line when this rig is used to float down a berley trail.

Main line

Ball sinker to suit current

Main line

Blood knot

Blood knot

First hook through eye

Free swinging hook

Tie a half hitch around tail

Main line

Ball sinker to suit current

Blood knot

Hook through eye

BAIT FISHING

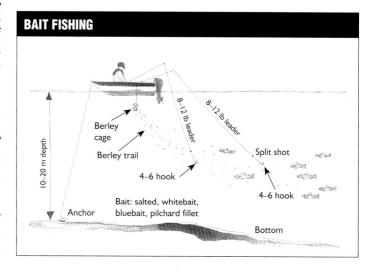

10-20 m depth

8-12 lb leader

8-12 lb leader

Berley cage

Berley trail

Split shot

4-6 hook

4-6 hook

Anchor

Bait: salted, whitebait, bluebait, pilchard fillet

Bottom

RIGS

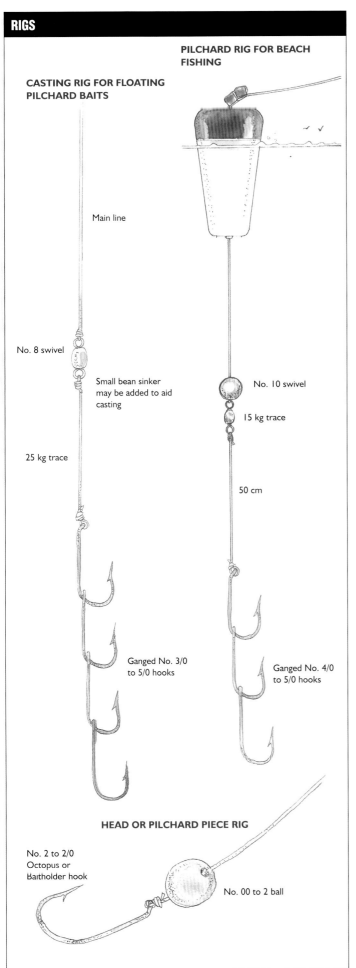

CASTING RIG FOR FLOATING PILCHARD BAITS

PILCHARD RIG FOR BEACH FISHING

Main line

No. 8 swivel

Small bean sinker may be added to aid casting

25 kg trace

No. 10 swivel

15 kg trace

50 cm

Ganged No. 3/0 to 5/0 hooks

Ganged No. 4/0 to 5/0 hooks

HEAD OR PILCHARD PIECE RIG

No. 2 to 2/0 Octopus or Baitholder hook

No. 00 to 2 ball

SWING RIG: PILCHARD

1. Pin the pillie in the side about here.

2. Make sure the hook is really well exposed.

3. Finish with two half hitches.

Snapper love pilchard baits and pilchard berley.

PISTOL SHRIMP

Also, known as nippers or green nippers, these shrimps are very good bait for estuarine fish including bream, whiting, mulloway, flathead and flounder will all feed enthusiastically on these baits. The biggest issue with these baits is the difficulty in collecting enough to use when you have a solid fishing session.

They occur right around Australia, and are mostly found in estuaries.

LOCATING

Pistol shrimp prefer hard structure such as rocks or timber close to the intertidal zones in estuaries and in rock/sand pools at low tide. They also frequent sea grass areas and especially where there are rocks or timber that they can get under for shelter. Turning over rocks etc. in these areas will often give up a shrimp or two for bait.

CATCHING AND HANDLING

They are like crabs around low tide rock pools etc. in that they will hold under rocks where there is some residue water left for them to hole up in. Turning over rocks or timber in these and other pools at low tide will often yield a shrimp or two as well as small crabs that are also excellent bait for similar estuarine fish.

Be careful of their large nipper claw when picking them up as they can give a painful bite. Place them in a bucket of fresh saltwater or wet seaweed, an aerator will help keep them alive as will replenishing the water and keeping them in the shade as much as possible.

These shrimps are like freshwater yabbies in that they will continually crawl under some sort of nearby cover given half a chance, so try and fish them over clear bottom areas, under a float or out of a drifting boat.

RIGGING

Because pistol shrimps are generally small and rarely greater than 50 mm in length, they are best fished using lighter weight hooks that can present the bait in a natural manner. The size of the hook should match the size of the bait, this would normally be a #6 t0 #4 hook, either long shank or suicide.

Thread the shrimp tail first onto the hook and run the hook right up the tail section and out where the tail meets the body. This will allow the shrimp to remain straight on the hook and present naturally to the fish.

Finding mulloway on quality electronics can be far easier than getting them to bite.

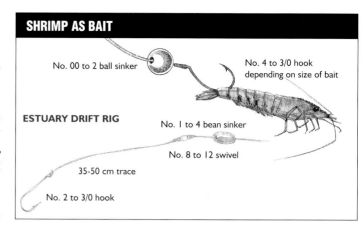

SHRIMP AS BAIT

No. 00 to 2 ball sinker

No. 4 to 3/0 hook depending on size of bait

ESTUARY DRIFT RIG

No. I to 4 bean sinker

No. 8 to I2 swivel

35-50 cm trace

No. 2 to 3/0 hook

The end result 15.2kg of mulloway taken on light bream gear.

RIGGED ON HOOK

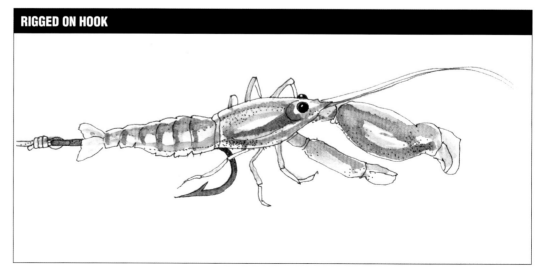

PRANS

One of the most popular and successful baits saltwater anglers can use, fresh or frozen, especially for anglers targeting estuarine fish species. They are a key food source for a large variety of fish and as such make an ideal everyday/multi species bait.

There are several prawn species in Australia, many of those used and bought frozen by anglers are school prawns, of which there are a variety of species. They all make excellent bait.

LOCATING

Fresh prawns can be gathered in varying quantities in most estuaries, and especially so in warmer climate areas. At certain times of the year, during the warmer months, and at new moon or dark of the moon phase each month, prawns are more active and available.

During certain times of the year, prawns make 'runs' out to sea from various estuaries and at these times it is possible, using hand nets and torches during the night, to catch enough prawns not only for use as bait, but for a meal fit for a king.

During 'non-run' times, smaller quantities of live prawns can be taken with cast nets in northern Australia along sand flats where there are weed banks, along gutters and drop-offs in estuaries or creek mouths, or along beach edges.

In temperate areas, the use of a fine mesh hand net, or drag net and bright lights searching likely areas often supplies enough fresh prawns for a fishing session.

CATCHING

Dragging likely areas with a prawn drag net or using a fine hand net mostly at night, when prawns are most active is the most productive method

to get a supply of baits. Alternatively, in popular tourist fishing areas, bait and tackle shops sell live prawns.

While live prawns (or any bait for that matter) are preferred, many recreational anglers usually purchase packets of frozen prawns for their convenience.

HANDLING AND STORAGE

Live prawns are best kept in aerated tanks with fresh seawater, the water they are held in should be a constant temperature and shaded to keep the prawns alive. Failing an aerated container, the use of a lidded Styrofoam esky or cooler that is located out of the sun will do for a fishing session.

Like most small baits, care when handling goes a long way to ensuring the prawns are strong and active when it comes time to use them.

If you do manage to catch more baits than you immediately need, fresh prawns can be frozen in containers with saltwater for a later stage. If these baits are frozen before they have had time to 'go off' they will be in perfect condition for use once defrosted.

When using pre-packaged frozen prawns, it is critical to select the best you can buy, look for prawns that are clean and green looking in the packet, aren't broken and of varying sizes. If the prawns are black around the heads and carapace area then avoid them as they won't be as attractive to the fish or remain on the hook for long when fishing. When buying frozen prawns only let defrost what you intend to use for bait and berley in any given session, never refreeze defrosted prawns unless you only intend to use them in berley at another time, and never as bait.

RIGGING

There are two ways to present prawns, either as full baits in a natural presentation, whether dead or alive, or as peeled prawns. Prawns just like any baits are most successful when presented as naturally as possible and fish, especially wily, shy fish such as bream, are far more receptive to prawns presented as they expect to see one in the wild. Straight and full bodied on the hook, peeled prawn baits on hooks will catch fish, but if you're after the bigger, wiser fish, then well-presented whole, live or dead prawns will be the better option.

Live prawns need to be hooked so they can remain alive and swim and kick so they look

PRAWNS AS BAIT

Where found: Nearly everywhere there is saltwater.

Gather or catch them: Use prawn scoops, drag nets and throw nets. The type of net or device you use will depend on your state Fisheries regulations.

Storing: If you are going to keep them live, get yourself a reliable aerator or continually keep changing the water, otherwise they will die very quickly. They can be frozen if you intend using them on a later trip. Depending on the type of prawn some don't refreeze well. It's a good idea to take off their heads before doing so as this will stop them turning black.

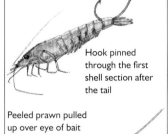

Hook pinned through the first shell section after the tail

Peeled prawn pulled up over eye of bait keeper hook

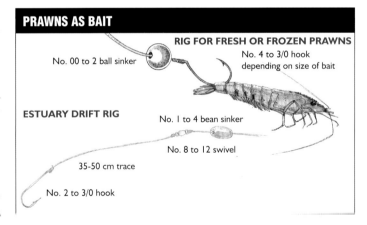

PRAWNS AS BAIT

RIG FOR FRESH OR FROZEN PRAWNS

No. 00 to 2 ball sinker

No. 4 to 3/0 hook depending on size of bait

ESTUARY DRIFT RIG

No. 1 to 4 bean sinker

No. 8 to 12 swivel

35-50 cm trace

No. 2 to 3/0 hook

natural, and the best way to do this is with a single light hook through the tail section with the prawn facing away from the hook.

The key to hooking dead prawns is to also make sure the bait is presented naturally and straight on the hook.

Casting a net for prawns at Rockhampton. it is all about getting fresh bait.

SALTWATER YABBIES

This is another very popular bait for estuarine species. It is also known as a Bass yabby or pink nipper in different states. It is one of the best baits going for those anglers chasing school mulloway, bream, whiting, flathead, flounder, drummer and trevally.

The downside of this bait is that they can give you a decent nip with that over-sized claw, and small fish tend to pick at them as well as the larger target fish. This can lead to losing quite a few baits when little pickers are about.

onto the dry sand or into the sieve. Any extracted yabbies are then dropped into a bucket containing saltwater.

HANDLING AND STORAGE

These baits, despite their menacing claws are quite fragile and should be handling carefully so they remain intact and alive. Pick them up lightly and make sure you avoid their large nipper in the process. Like all live baits that breathe in water, it is important that you oxygenate the water in the bucket regularly, especially if you have several yabbies in there. An aerated bait bucket is a better proposition if you're collecting

Nippers or 'one arm bandits' can be a hot bait for bream. Their only drawback is that they are easily removed by non-target species.

LOCATING

Intertidal sand banks and flats are the preferred habitat for these baits, they bury themselves across these flats and their presence is noted by often vast areas of burrows and tell-tale holes in the sand at low tide.

COLLECTING

A yabby pump, bait bucket and a floating sieve (if pumping in shallow water) are all the tools you need for collecting these top baits. The pump tube is placed over the selected hole and pumped so that the yabby and sand is lifted, the contents of the pump are them expelled

numerous baits for a later fishing session rather than immediately after collection, ensure you remove any dead yabbies to avoid them turning the water putrid and killing the other yabbies.

As with all live baits, keep shaded to avoid overheating, and ensure that you aren't replacing water that is a noticeably different temperature, as this variance can be enough to shock and kill the baits.

RIGGING

Because saltwater yabbies are

quite fragile and lightweight, it pays to use small and lightweight hooks that match the size of the bait being used. Large yabbies can be fished with the hook going in at the tail and exiting at the top of the body in the tail section. Smaller baits are best used by threading the hook into the tail and exiting out on the underneath side at around

three or four tail segments in. Both these methods present the bait naturally and keep it alive to attract more fish. The sinker weight to hold the bait on the bottom is all that is required, and a slow looping cast instead of a sharp quick cast will help to keep the bait on the hook during casting these top baits.

ESTUARY RIG 1

This is a common rig employed using nippers of yabbies for estuary perch. The bubble fl oat is transparent and weighted with water to enable casting. The hook should be a medium to long shank and the size varies to suit the bait. Most anglers will fi nd a hook about No. 2 to No. 4 will cover most situations, although larger hooks can be used.

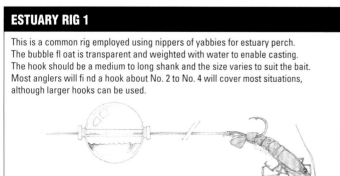

ESTUARY RIG 2

ESTUARY DRIFT & CASTING RIGS

No. 1 to 3 bean or bug sinker

30-50cm

No. 8 to 12 swivel

Main line

No. 6 to 2 Baitholder or Long Shank hook

BREAM RIG ALSO USED FOR JETTY & ROCK FISHING

No. 0 to 2 ball sinker

No. 4 to 2 hook

Double half hitch

Hook comes out of the head of the pink nipper

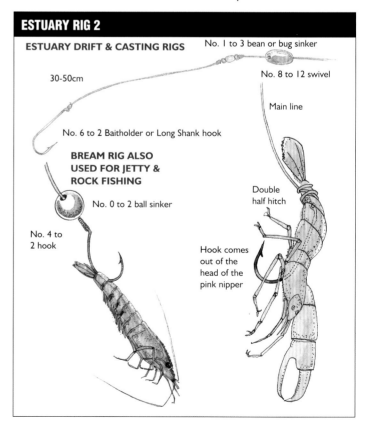

SANDWORMS

Sandworms, also called squirt worms, pump worms and rag worms, are one of the most popular baits for anglers chasing whiting, flounder and finicky bream in estuaries. They are also prime bait for other fish such as garfish and mullet that require small hooks and small baits. They can be found Australia wide, but are most commonly collected by anglers along the east coast.

LOCATING

They inhabit open sand and mudflats and their small domed mounds across these flats is the best indicator these top baits are about. Usually when you come across a good location, these little domes will be quite extensive and most evident on low tides, and the lower the better as this will allow you to collect in areas not normally available and as such be more productive.

COLLECTING

The best and easiest method of collection is to use a yabby pump. This is place over the domed hole and pumped out onto the sand, the pumped sand is then sorted and the sandworms collected. A fine floating sieve can be useful if you are pumping where there is still some water over the holes, the pumped sand is ejected into the sieve to catch any worms present.

HANDLING AND STORAGE

Sandworms are extremely fragile and often break into small pieces with even moderate handling. As with other saltwater worms, delicate handling and touching as little as possible are the key. A fresh wash in saltwater and then into a container of damp seaweed or saltwater, and stored in the shade is the best handling for an immediate fishing session.

Because of their fragility and susceptibility to longer term storage, it makes sense to only collect what you will need for your immediate use.

RIGGING

Because of their small size and fragile nature, sandworms are best rigged on small, lightweight baitholder hooks. They should be presented naturally and not bunched on the hook with an enticing tail left dangling. When targeting small mouthed fish such as mullet and gars, or even luderick at times, it is possible to use small and broken pieces of worm on small hooks.

Fishing the shallows.

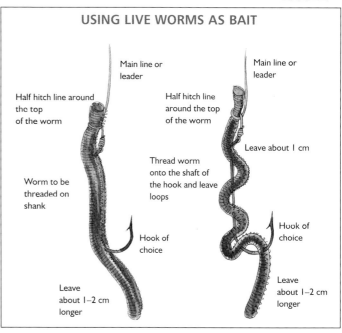

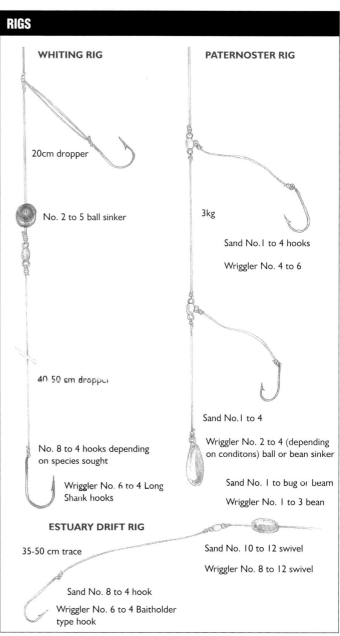

SCRUBWORMS

While every baitfisher at some time or another fish with garden worms, fewer are aware of the fantastic fishing that can be had by using their bigger cousins, scrubworms. These large worms can in fact be almost too large to fish effectively at times for certain fish species. Anglers chasing trout and redfin etc should look for 'scrubbies' ranging from 60 to 100mm in length for the best results and to cover most sportfish species.

LOCATING

Most dedicated anglers that fish with scrubworms have areas where they can 'dig their own' baits, these areas often feature rich, moist and loamy soils and often along watercourses. Anywhere that there is a lot or rotting vegetation around slower flowing rivers and billabongs can be prime scrubworm country.

A word of warning though, when searching for and digging scrubworms it should be recognised that you are impacting on a natural environment, and as a responsible angler, it falls back to you to fill in any holes you dig so that the area isn't destroyed visually or environmentally.

COLLECTING

Modern anglers who are often time poor, simply purchase their scrubworms from reputable tackle stores and bait supply shops. And considering the possible impact of searching about and digging holes in search of these baits, that makes good sense in saving time and protecting the environment. Professional bait collectors have a real vested interest in making sure their bait collecting areas are well managed and cared for so they do keep producing into the future.

HANDLING AND STORAGE

Scrubworms will keep alive for long periods given the right conditions and kept in a cool place. They are stored in largish Styrofoam vegetable boxes with drainage holes to allow any excess water to drain away to avoid the worms drowning. Add good loam soil and composted material and keep covered with a damp hessian bag on top. So, long as the bag is kept damp and the container out of any direct heat and in a cool place, the scrubworms will live for a long period. These larger containers are ideal as storage containers, and when a fishing trip is planned, simply transferring the required bait from these into a smaller foam esky containing some loamy soil.

RIGGING

There are several ways to rig these prime baits. When fishing a single worm across shelving lake beds and flooded lake flats the standard method involves the use of a single hook passed down through the worm so that its body is threaded with the fishing line before the hook is exposed about two thirds of the way towards the worm's tail. The alternative to this is to use a single, smaller hook passed once through the worm at one end. This allows for more freedom to wriggle and twist, which attracts the attention of fish other than just by smell. This hooking method is most often used when anglers are baitcasting streams and allowing the worm to float and drift with the current. This fishing method can also be used in conjunction with a yarn strike indicator or a light-weight quill float if necessary. Another method involves using two small hooks with the top hook snelled to the line and a dropper of line then running down to another small hook at the other end of the worm. This two-hook rig allows for fish that are just lifting and playing with the bait to be hooked more effectively.

Scrubworm

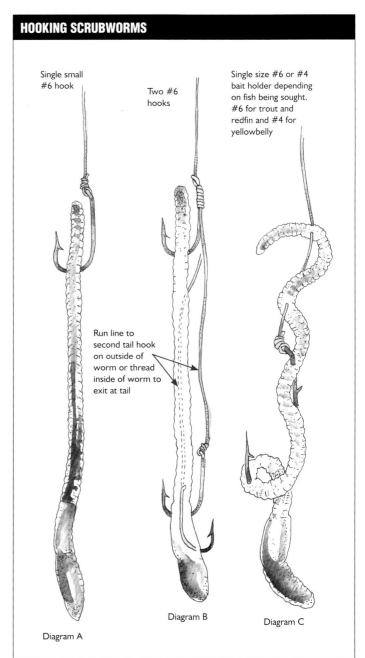

HOOKING SCRUBWORMS

Single small #6 hook

Two #6 hooks

Single size #6 or #4 bait holder depending on fish being sought. #6 for trout and redfin and #4 for yellowbelly

Run line to second tail hook on outside of worm or thread inside of worm to exit at tail

Diagram A

Diagram B

Diagram C

SCRUBWORM RIGS

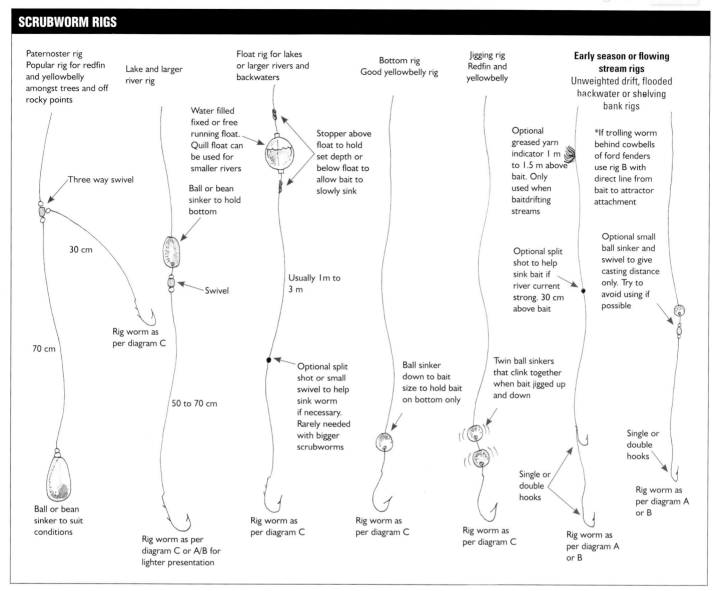

Paternoster rig
Popular rig for redfin and yellowbelly amongst trees and off rocky points

Three way swivel

30 cm

70 cm

Ball or bean sinker to suit conditions

Lake and larger river rig

Water filled fixed or free running float. Quill float can be used for smaller rivers

Ball or bean sinker to hold bottom

Swivel

Rig worm as per diagram C

50 to 70 cm

Rig worm as per diagram C or A/B for lighter presentation

Float rig for lakes or larger rivers and backwaters

Stopper above float to hold set depth or below float to allow bait to slowly sink

Usually 1m to 3 m

Optional split shot or small swivel to help sink worm if necessary. Rarely needed with bigger scrubworms

Rig worm as per diagram C

Bottom rig
Good yellowbelly rig

Ball sinker down to bait size to hold bait on bottom only

Rig worm as per diagram C

Jigging rig
Redfin and yellowbelly

Optional greased yarn indicator 1 m to 1.5 m above bait. Only used when baitdrifting streams

Optional split shot to help sink bait if river current strong. 30 cm above bait

Twin ball sinkers that clink together when bait jigged up and down

Single or double hooks

Rig worm as per diagram C

Early season or flowing stream rigs
Unweighted drift, flooded backwater or shelving bank rigs

*If trolling worm behind cowbells of ford fenders use rig B with direct line from bait to attractor attachment

Optional small ball sinker and swivel to give casting distance only. Try to avoid using if possible

Single or double hooks

Rig worm as per diagram A or B

Rig worm as per diagram A or B

When using scrubworms, only the minimum sinker weight should ever be used to deliver, present or hold the bait in the strikezone. These are big baits and the fish will often pick them up, taste them, suck on them and move about quite a lot before swallowing them. Only the very largest of fish will generally be able to inhale a larger scrubworm straight off, and as such, more angling finesse is often required when fishing these baits.

When fishing the lake flats or flooded river margins or backwaters the angler should endeavour to fish an open bail if possible to allow the fish to pick up and run and then stop and eat the bait before setting the hook.

Paternoster rigs are a favourite setup for scrubworms at times, particularly when the bait is being used to target redfin and yellowbelly around snags and at these times a tight line from bait to rod is the preferred setup. These more aggressive fish will generally hit the bait far harder than trout.

Smaller scrubworms are effective at times when fished under bubble floats and these rigs are often employed earlier in the trout season when there is some colour about in the lakes and rivers.

Single scrubworms can also be slow trolled behind cowbells and ford fenders, similar to mudeyes, and for the most part are more effective than mudeyes

for this method. The wriggling and twisting of a larger, single worm through the water seems to be very attractive, especially to trout in the big dams.

SCRUBWORMS

Storage
Scrubworms can be stored for some time without dying in large containers such as styrofoam vegetable boxes with drainage holes to remove excess water. If kept cool with good loam soil and old composted material and covered with damp hessian they will last for months.

Time of Year
Scrubworms fish well throughout the year but fish far better for trout in rivers and lakes at the start of the season when there is some fresh flowing.
Big redfin love scrubworms through the middle of winter in many lakes when fished on paternoster rigs. Redfin and native fish will eat scrubworms throughout the year.

Line Weight
Six pound test is fine for most trout and redfin fishing using single scrubworms under floats and on running sinkers in lakes and streams. It is worth beefing the line up to 10 lb and beyond when fishing heavier paternoster rigs amongst snags for redfin and natives.

Hooks
Hooks will vary depending on fish being sought rather than bait size when using scrubworms.

Target Fish
Trout, redfin, Murray cod, Macquarie perch, yellow belly. If targeting river blackfish then smaller scrubworms can and should be used.

SILVER WHITING

Silver whiting (*Sillago ciliata*), also known as school or eastern whiting can be found from Cape York in Queensland and along the entire east coast, and as far south as the east coast of Tasmania. They are best known to snapper anglers who purchase them frozen for bait, mostly in Port Phillip Bay and Western Port.

The above species is often confused with *Sillago bassensis*, which is also commonly known as a silver or southern whiting. This species ranges from Western Australia, along the southern coast to Western Port in Victoria. This species is most easily recognised by the other because of its 'tiger stripes' along the dorsal area of its body. For all intents and purposes, both species make quality baits and there is no need for differentiation.

LOCATING

They are found mostly over sandy areas, reef and weed patches where they can be caught for bait or a feed. Although their smallish average size often means they are more likely destined to be used as fresh or frozen bait for snapper and gummy shark. Depending on which of the two species are targeted, they can be found inshore or in tidal areas, or out to depths of 100 metres.

They are often caught in large numbers by commercial fishermen.

CATCHING

Like all whiting species, they both respond well to berleying and traditional whiting rigs and baits. Typical fishing setups consist of rods rated between 2 – 4kg and matched to 2500 series reels, spooled with 2-3 kg braid and a slightly heavier fluorocarbon or mono leader. Silver whiting have small mouths, so long shank hooks in sizes 8, 10 or 12 are the best bet.

Most anglers buy these baits frozen in vacuum sealed bags,

for a greater hook up rate on snapper due to the bait being swallowed more easily and not spat out as is the case with whole baits.

As with all baits, ensuring the hook barbs are clear and exposed from the bait goes a long way to ensuring a successful hook up rate.

Gummy sharks and snapper are two prime targets when using silver whiting as bait

and for convenience. Especially when using them for use as bait for larger fish. This is the most efficient method to attaining baits of a consistent size for snapper and other target fish when rigged whole.

RIGGING

Silver Whiting have a tough skin that is covered in scales, this toughness makes them a great big fish bait for snapper and gummy shark. Depending on the size of the bait, they can be used whole, cut in half or rigged with the head removed. For whole and baits with heads removed, a snelled, two hook rig is preferred, while a cut half bait using a single hook often allows

SWING RIG: SILVER WHITING

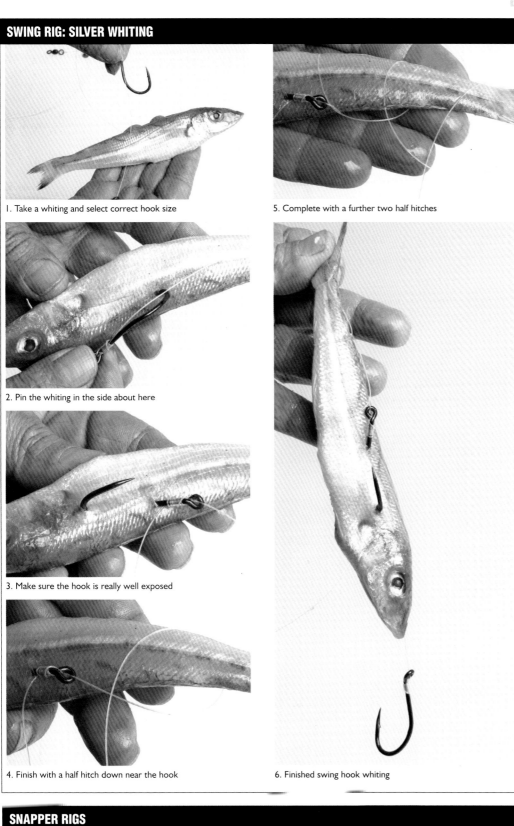

1. Take a whiting and select correct hook size

2. Pin the whiting in the side about here

3. Make sure the hook is really well exposed

4. Finish with a half hitch down near the hook

5. Complete with a further two half hitches

6. Finished swing hook whiting

SNAPPER RIGS

Running sinker to suit conditions

swivel

Longline knots holds second hook in potion. Thsi is a great rig for whole squid, strip bait and silver whiting

SNAPPER RIGS

There are two types of rigs used commonly around Whyalla, the running paternoster and the fixed paternoster. Both call for quick change of sinkers as the current requires.

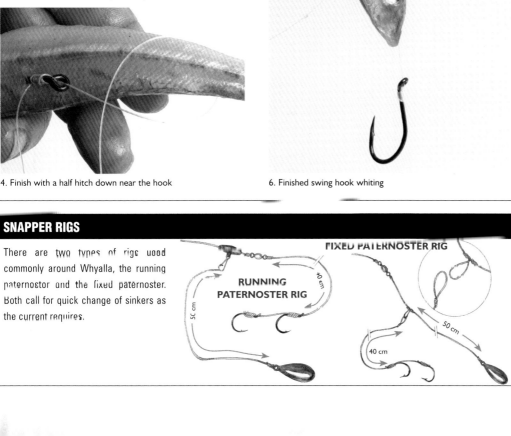

FIXED PATERNOSTER RIG

RUNNING PATERNOSTER RIG

40 cm

50 cm

50 cm

40 cm

SLIMY MACKEREL

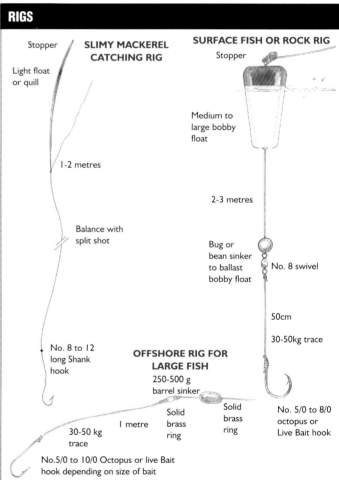

Slimy mackerel, alongside yellowtail, would be rated as the top two live baits for large predatory fish. Slimy mackerel frequent much of the temperate Australian coast and wherever they are found they offer fantastic light line fishing and top notch live or cut baits.

Depending on the size of the mackerel, they are productive baits for any predatory fish including marlin.

They are found in all Australian waters, plus in japan, but they are most common in temperate waters in the southern half of Australia.

LOCATING

They are a schooling offshore species that will frequently venture into large bays and harbours and frequent areas around jetties and piers where young and old anglers enjoy catching them. They frequent known offshore bait grounds and can be berleyed up or located with sounders if hanging deep.

CATCHING

Light lines and rods, and small hooks baited with small pieces of tuna etc. will work on these seemingly always hungry fish. Berleying out at sea over the bait grounds or around jetties and piers will usually bring these fish around and get them feeding if they are in the vicinity.

A berley made up of wet bread and a few mashed pieces of pilchard or oily tuna will work well in a berley bucket, or alternatively a small tuna carcass rubbing against pier pylons or occasionally scraped with a knife is also effective.

Small bait jigs drop into a school of mackerel working around a pier or fish deep offshore to sounded schools can give multiple bait fish at a time. Once the bait fish are feeding actively, which is often, multiple hooked jigs are very productive.

HANDLING AND STORING

Slimies are very susceptible to over handling, so if your intention is to use them for live bait it helps not to physically handle them but shake or flip them off the hook and into a very aerated bait tank, these little speedsters require lots of oxygen to stay alive so keep this in mind when you're collecting for live bait. They will travel well if handling is kept to a minimum and they get lots of oxygen in the bait tank.

RIGGING

There is no bad way to use 'slimies' as bait, but the preferred option, and where they really shine is as live bait, depending on their size, there are very few fish that won't eat them given half-a-chance. Medium to large mackerel are top live baits for Spanish mackerel, mulloway, kingfish, large tuna and numerous other larger predatory fish. Mackerel also make fantastic strip and cut baits for smaller fish such as snapper, bream, flathead etc.

Slimy mackerel don't freeze well, so a good bait tank or an ice slurry is best to keep them alive or fresh during a fishing session.

Bridle rigged slimy mackerel

RIGS

SLIMY MACKEREL CATCHING RIG

Stopper

Light float or quill

1-2 metres

Balance with split shot

No. 8 to 12 long Shank hook

SURFACE FISH OR ROCK RIG

Stopper

Medium to large bobby float

2-3 metres

Bug or bean sinker to ballast bobby float

No. 8 swivel

50cm

30-50kg trace

No. 5/0 to 8/0 octopus or Live Bait hook

OFFSHORE RIG FOR LARGE FISH

250-500 g barrel sinker

Solid brass ring

Solid brass ring

1 metre

30-50 kg trace

No.5/0 to 10/0 Octopus or live Bait hook depending on size of bait

---

UNWEIGHTED LIVE BAIT RIG

Live baitfish can be slow trolled around bait balls and pinnacles. More often though they are simply lowered down into the water column to a desired depth and then moved slowly away from the area, appearing as a straggler. It is often necessary when fishing this way to put a large ball sinker on the line to hold the baitfish at the required depth. Hook size should be chosen to suit the bait, and the hook is located either in front of the first dorsal fin or, as is the case with slimy mackerel, through the flesh nostril on the top jaw.

SQUID

Squid are not only a very popular bait, but also an extremely popular table fare. So often it's a toss-up between catching these for bait or dinner.

They are commonly caught at times in estuaries, bays and offshore, but also available in packets from tackle outlets.

There aren't many fish species that won't take a well-presented squid bait. One of the main benefits of these baits is that they stay on the hook and aren't removed by picker fish like some softer baits.

LOCATING

Squid can be found in deep bays, harbours and in deeper water around headlands, offshore reefs and bait grounds. Generally, if you locate schools of baitfish in any of the areas above, you're likely to encounter feeding squid because they are quite voracious. They are attracted to lights at nights and therefore can often be found around deepwater jetties and piers where they feed on the attracted baitfish.

CATCHING

Squid are very aggressive hunters and will attack multi prong lures that are cast and retrieved, or floated under a bobby cork when there is some wave action to impart some attractive movement to the lure. These multi-pronged lures have evolved greatly in recent years, especially now that fishing for squid for the table has become so popular.

Squid will also take fish baits

Selection of squid jigs

rigged onto specialist squid jigs or even on standard hooks, baited with fish under bobby cork floats.

When squid are, thick and milling around, it is even possible to catch them using landing nets or spears.

HANDLING AND STORAGE

Squid don't remain alive long after capture, so if you're intending to use them as live bait, it often pays to have your mulloway, kingfish or specialist outfit ready to hook the fresh squid straight out of the water and get it back out there. Keep in mind that squid will squirt a jet of black ink as a defence mechanism when being lifted out of the water, so be ready for this to avoid being 'inked'. A bucket or container with some saltwater will allow you to time to swap rods and get the fresh squid rigged onto your fishing outfit.

If you're fishing for squid for the table, or for dead or cut bait, then the most important thing is to treat them carefully to get the best from them and keep them looking good for later use.

Squid change colour to white when in contact with freshwater,

so ice boxes, or even ice and saltwater slurry's will have the same effect. Well aerated bait tanks on boats will allow you to keep them alive longer, or placing them into a plastic bag with saltwater and sealing it before dropping onto ice will keep the dead squid looking good rather than turning white.

While it isn't necessarily an issue using cut squid that has turned white for bait, fresher is always best, so whether you are buying fresh dead squid or frozen dead squid, always look for the bait that doesn't look watery, white, or off-white in colour, fresh and good quality squid, whether for eating or bait, will have good colour and the finely dotted surface skin intact.

RIGGING

There are many ways to rig squid, the size of the bait and the intended target fish will usually determine how many hooks are used. Large squid are usually cut into sections to make them a more appropriate size for bait. Long tentacles are often used and rigged singularly as larger baits, while smaller pieces are more suitable for paternoster rigs for offshore drifting for general bottom fish species.

Squid take a range of jig colours

RIGGING SQUID BAITS FOR MULLOWAY

Expert mulloway and snapper fisherman Marl Shean showed Geoff Wilson this method of rigging a small squid (three or more to the kilogram), to make two baits, for mulloway

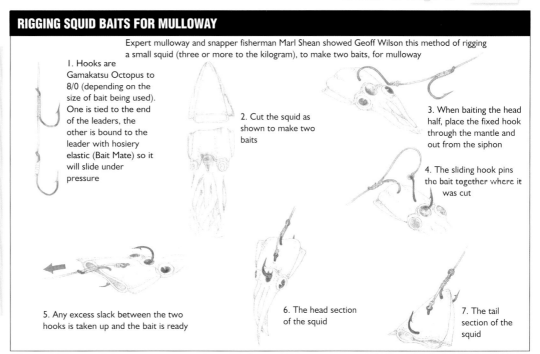

1. Hooks are Gamakatsu Octopus to 8/0 (depending on the size of bait being used). One is tied to the end of the leaders, the other is bound to the leader with hosiery elastic (Bait Mate) so it will slide under pressure

2. Cut the squid as shown to make two baits

3. When baiting the head half, place the fixed hook through the mantle and out from the siphon

4. The sliding hook pins the bait together where it was cut

5. Any excess slack between the two hooks is taken up and the bait is ready

6. The head section of the squid

7. The tail section of the squid

SQUID

If you are catching squid, remember to leave them in the water, or point them away from you, until they have discharged all their defensive ink.

Big kingfish, snapper and mulloway love squid baits.

RIGS

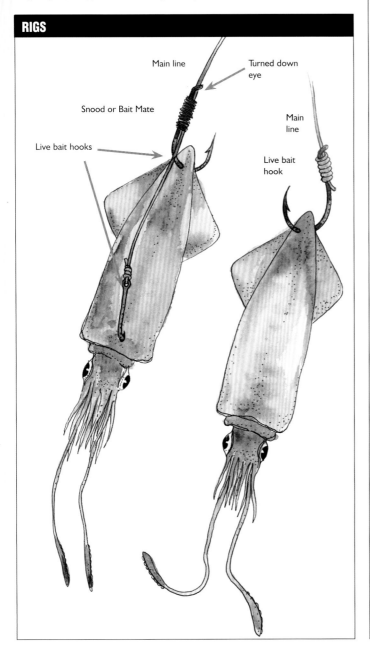

Main line

Turned down eye

Snood or Bait Mate

Main line

Live bait hooks

Live bait hook

RIGS

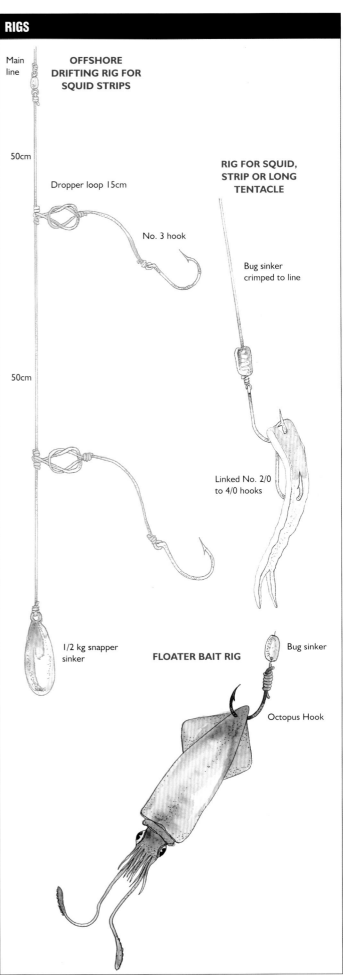

Main line

OFFSHORE DRIFTING RIG FOR SQUID STRIPS

50cm

Dropper loop 15cm

No. 3 hook

RIG FOR SQUID, STRIP OR LONG TENTACLE

Bug sinker crimped to line

50cm

Linked No. 2/0 to 4/0 hooks

1/2 kg snapper sinker

FLOATER BAIT RIG

Bug sinker

Octopus Hook

TUNA

Small tuna species, especially bonito, striped tuna, frigate mackerel and mackerel tuna, all make ideal bait and berley. Few fish baits have the general appeal to other fish species than fresh and oily tuna.

Whether it be small cubes of fresh tuna used to catch yellowtail or slimy mackerel from a pier, or rigged whole for chasing marlin, tuna make top bait.

LOCATING

All the fish that fall into this category, school up, so when you get onto them, it's likely you will catch a few. They appear at certain times of the year in various locations and are often caught by trolling appropriate lures on the way out to, or back from reef areas, or by locating surface feeding sea birds. When you get onto a big school of these fish good bags can be harvested for fresh and frozen baits. Tuna are caught mostly in deep water areas around headlands, offshore ridges, along ocean current lines both along and offshore.

CATCHING

As already mentioned, trolling at faster speeds using feathered lures, or smallish flashy metal slices or cheap skirted lures attached to heavy cord to allow the angler to get the

fish in quickly and catch more is productive, as is locating a school of fish and casting lures using standard fishing tackle. This second method is more fun, but it also takes far longer to get a decent amount (unless they are very small fish) if you're specifically chasing fish for live bait.

It's important to generally use a lure that can be retrieved very quickly (so a high gear ratio reel is important) to entice these speedsters to get excited and hit your lure.

HANDLING AND STORAGE

Despite the best modern live bait tanks, captured tuna tends to die very quickly, so the best bet is to treat them with respect and get them onto ice straight away if they are to be used as bait that same day, or if they are being caught for future use, an ice slurry of one third seawater and two thirds ice will keep the caught fish fresh until they can be frozen later.

RIGGING

If small tuna is to be used as live bait for large pelagic fish, then it is imperative they are caught and rigged at or very near the offshore fishing grounds so they don't die. Most of these baits when used whole are dead fish freshly caught and in an ice slurry for the days fishing. And these large pelagic baits are

Todd Fisher caught this yellowfin tuna on a cube.

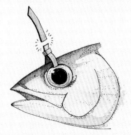
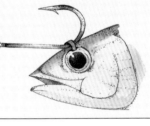

LIVE BAIT TROLLING

Towing live baits is a proven method of catching big fish. Marlin, sailfish, tuna, dolphin fish (mahi mahi), yellowtail kingfish, cobia, mackerel, sharks and others will all fall for a trolled live bait. Baits like large slimy mackerel, large yellowtail, frigate mackerel, cowanyoung and striped tuna (skipjack) all work.

Historically, these baits were rigged using a bridle made of dacron or other strong thread which was tied to the hook and then passed through the eye socket or nose of the bait and was then looped back onto the hook and the bait dropped into the water. This remains a popular and effective method.

The quickest method of rigging these baits is to use a plastic electrical tie.

Live baits are usually trolled with the reel just in gear, with enough drag to stop an overrun when the hit comes and the predator fish is given time and line while it swallows the bait. Once the big fish is presumed to have swallowed the bait the fish is struck and the fight is on.

When a quick rig is required to troll a bait the simple answer is to hook the bait through the nose, side to side.

This rig works perfectly well, but the baits don't last as long, though they last an hour or more which can be plenty. They can also be ripped off the hook at the strike, though this is rare and applies mostly to slimy mackerel.

Steps

1 The tie is cut at 45 degrees to give it a sharp point.

2 Pass the tie through the top of the bait's eye socket and then close it and pull tight.

3 Once tight, snip off the tag end.

4 The hook is slipped under the tie and the bait is ready to troll.

generally bridle rigged in various ways to make them skip or swim when being trolled.

Whole dead baits can also be used when drift fishing for sharks.

Cut cubed or strip pieces of tuna baits make very attractive and successful baits

when targeting popular bottom feeding table fish, and the flesh and frames of the cut up small tuna are also an important ingredient for anglers using a berley trail for smaller live baitfish or to attract larger tuna such as yellowfin up the berley trail to the angler's small live bait rigs.

CUBING

Time your cubes to enter water at a set time interval. Normally, when the cube disappears from view another is tossed in

LURE TROLLING PATTERN FOR TUNA

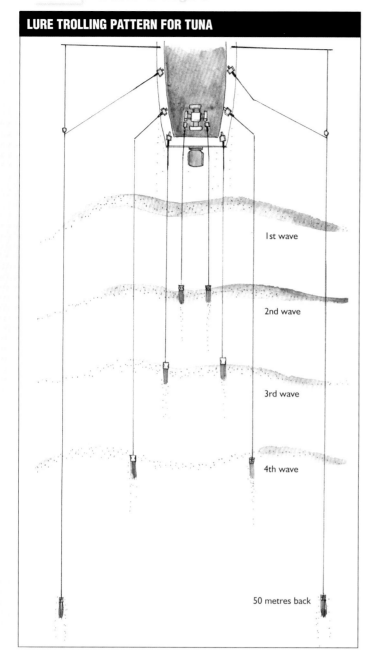

1st wave

2nd wave

3rd wave

4th wave

50 metres back

A stunning Northern Blue Tuna that was caught while harassing a school of small garfish.

RIGS

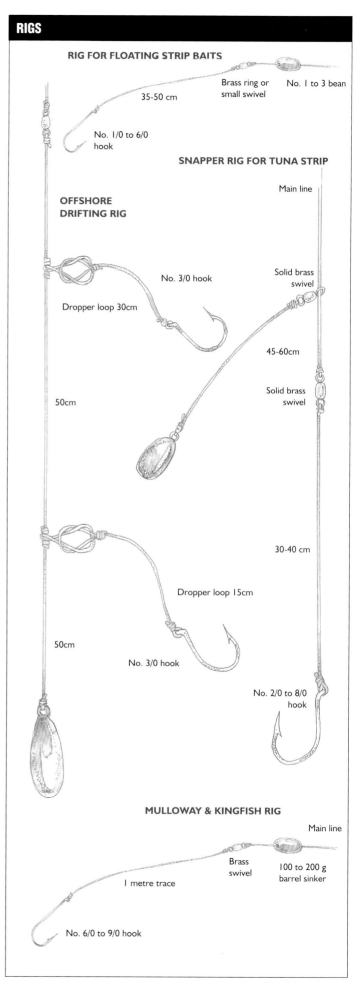

RIG FOR FLOATING STRIP BAITS

Brass ring or small swivel

No. 1 to 3 bean

35-50 cm

No. 1/0 to 6/0 hook

SNAPPER RIG FOR TUNA STRIP

Main line

OFFSHORE DRIFTING RIG

No. 3/0 hook

Dropper loop 30cm

Solid brass swivel

45-60cm

Solid brass swivel

50cm

30-40 cm

Dropper loop 15cm

50cm

No. 3/0 hook

No. 2/0 to 8/0 hook

MULLOWAY & KINGFISH RIG

Main line

Brass swivel

100 to 200 g barrel sinker

1 metre trace

No. 6/0 to 9/0 hook

WHITEBAIT

One of the most popular and often used baits for numerous species including bream, flathead, small mulloway, flounder, trevally, salmon, and several other species including trout and salmon in several freshwater lakes. It is used as bait in estuaries, surf and offshore. It not only makes a top bait but is also very productive when used in a berley mix.

They range from Kalbarri in Western Australia and around the southern waters and up to southern Queensland. They can be identified separately from hardyheads (which are often sold as whitebait) most easily with their single dorsal fin instead of two on hardyheads.

Either species are excellent bait however and used the same.

LOCATING

Whitebait can be found schooling along beaches, off estuary mouths and harbours where they can be netted or trapped if permissible in the area. Professional fishers also net them and fresh baits can be purchased where these fishers work in the northern and western states of Australia.

HANDLING

Most anglers tend to purchase pre-frozen packets of these baits unless they have ready access to freshly caught whitebait. As with all frozen baits, it often comes down to how the original baits have been handle before freezing, quality frozen whitebait should be shiny with clear eyes and no noticeable discolouration along the body and especially along the belly area. If the packets contain broken baits then reject them.

RIGGING

For saltwater fishing, try and purchase white bait that are of a reasonable length, over 80 mm at least so they can be rigged correctly and be attractive to larger fish. If you're chasing trout or salmon in freshwater, then smaller size whitebait that mimic the natural baitfish size in the lakes of around 60 to 70mm are fine.

As with most straight bodied baits, the key to successful rigging is to avoid twisting the bait or having it slide down and bunching on the hook. As with pilchards, rigging on ganged hooks with the top hook going through the eye ensures the bait lies straight and looks most enticing. Small baits used for trout and salmon can be fished using one hook only, and this hook is best placed through the eyes and using two baits at a time.

Hooked straight and drifted in an estuary of bay, or allowed to swing about in the surf on a paternoster rig, there are few more universally popular baits for saltwater fish than whitebait.

Profile of whitebait and frogmouth pilchard.

Frogmouth and whitebait presented on double hook and single hook.

There are literally hundreds of beaches along the Australian coastline from nothern Queensland and around the bottom of Australia and up to Shark Bay in WA.

DRIFTING & CASTING RIG

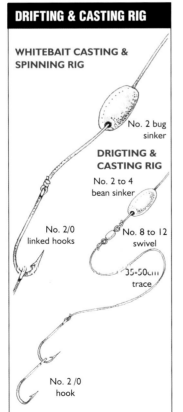

WHITEBAIT CASTING & SPINNING RIG

No. 2 bug sinker

DRIGTING & CASTING RIG

No. 2 to 4 bean sinker

No. 2/0 linked hooks

No. 8 to 12 swivel

35-50cm trace

No. 2 /0 hook

SINGLE AND DOUBLE HOOK RIGS

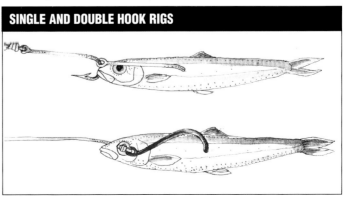

YELLOWTAIL

Alive or dead, swum whole or as cut bait, yellowtail or 'yakkas' as they are affectionately called, are one of the most frequent and best fish baits when chasing kingfish, various tunas, mulloway, snapper, tailor and flathead, or just about any predatory fish. They are sometimes referred to as yellowtail scad, scad, bung or chow in some regions. They range from Point Quobba in Western Australia, and all southern waters (although not common in Tasmania) and north as far as Bribie Island in southern Queensland.

They are also extremely abundant for both land based and offshore anglers to collect and use fresh which is a bonus.

LOCATING

These fish school in good numbers and tend to congregate around structure. They inhabit bays, estuaries, rocky coastline areas and offshore reefs out in deep water. They love structure such as jetties and wharfs etc. which makes them easy and fun targets for youngsters to catch, they hang around rocky headlands where they can be caught by land-based game anglers, and on bait grounds offshore where gamefisher's can collect fresh bait on the way out to chase large offshore pelagic fish, or bottom-bouncers can collect baits for reef fish.

COLLECTING

Wherever these bait fish are found, the best method to get them schooled up and eating your bait or jig is to berley them up. Bread and fish pulp work well to hold these fish around while you catch what you need for bait.

Light rods with light line and small baited hooks or bait jigs dropped down into the school should have enough baits quickly for a session.

HANDLING AND STORAGE

Yellowtail are very hardy, but they do need aerated water if you're intending to keep more than two or three in a bucket. Anglers fishing off headlands often take in blow up kiddie pools that they put seawater into at the fishing location and keep any yellowtail they catch alive in this. If you don't have an aerator then you will need to limit the amount of live baits you can keep alive in a bucket, and even so, you will need to replenish the water regularly at 30 minute intervals.

If your intention is to use them down track as dead baits, then storing them in a seawater ice slurry to keep them fresh for use or freezing.

RIGGING

There are many ways to use yellowtail as bait. One of the

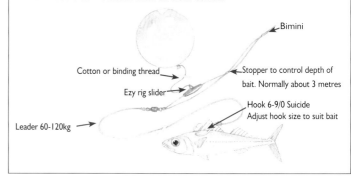

LIVE BAIT RIG FOR LAND BASED GAME FISHING

This is the staple live bait rig set up used to land based game fishing on the East Coast. Leader material is 60-120kg breaking strain and normally about 3 metres long. Hook size varies to suit baits, but 6/0-9/0 Suicide pattern hooks cover most baitfish.

Suicide hooks have an offset and this should be allowed for when setting the hook in a baitfish. With the bait in your hand check that when the hook is inserted the point will be angled towards the head of the baitfish. If the point is angled to the rear it will dig into the bait as it is swimming around. You usually only get one chance to burry the hook and if the point is embedded in the back of the bait there is a good chance you will miss a potential hook-up The connection between leader and main line is a good quality ball bearing game swivel, preferably black as shiny swivels have been know to attact bites from small toothies. A double leader is tied on the main line using a Bimini twist knot. Before the double is tied to the swivel, the strands are cut and an Ezi-rig slider threaded on to one of the double strands. A balloon is attached to the Ezi-rig slider either with binding thread or 1 monofilament. A Stopper knot is then tied over both strands of the double to control bait depth. So, even though your leader is say three metres, you may want to allow to Ezi-rig to run anopther couple of metres up the line, which subsequently allows the bait to swim 5 metres down the water column.

Bimini

Cotton or binding thread

Ezy rig slider

Stopper to control depth of bait. Normally about 3 metres

Hook 6-9/0 Suicide Adjust hook size to suit bait

Leader 60-120kg

Many varieties of pelagic fish, such as Red emperors are keyed into hunting live yellowtail baits.

most popular methods is to hook them lightly through the shoulder/back or nose area in front of the eyes, taking care to avoid hitting the spine which will kill the baitfish. Hook size is dependent on the size of the baitfish being used, and the intended target species. Dead yellowtail can be cut up and used in cubes, strips or whole, again, depending on size of the bait and target species. They are also suitable for use in berley, although other oilier fish such as slimy mackerel are more popular.

HOOK PLACEMENT POSITIONS

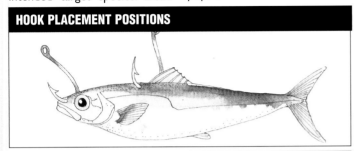

YELLOWTAIL (YAKKAS) USE LIVE OR DEAD

Where found: Yellowtail just love to hang around places where there is a combination of rocks or boulders, kelp and sand. They can also be found around wharfs, pylons, swing moorings, inshore and offshore reefs or just about anywhere there is a structure of some kind.

Gather or catch it: All you need to catch yellowtail is a hand line with a paternoster rig, number eight or ten long shanked hook, a small piece of either pilchard, tuna, chicken fillet or any other bait that has a bit of oil in it and a steady stream of berley. The trick to getting the fussy yellowtail to bite is to use pilchards as berley. For those of you that live in Queensland you could try using a cast net to catch your bait.

Storing: If you are going to keep them live you will either need to get yourself a reliable aerator or continually keep changing the water, otherwise they will die on you very quickly. Whole or filleted yellowtail can be stored in a plastic container in the freezer. If you wanted to you could sprinkle a bit of salt over them, but I find that they are just as good without it.

Bait jig used to hook yakkas for live bait.

RIGS

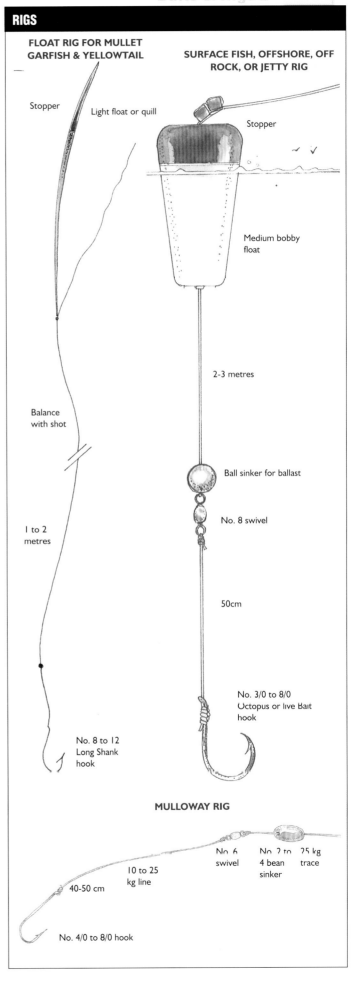

BAIT JIG RIGS

Many small baitfish school in large numbers for protection, garfish, slimy mackerel and yellowtails are perfect examples of this. And large schools of fish generally tend to be very competitive when it comes feeding, often it's every fish for themselves. And this feeding frenzy works in our favour when it comes to catching these smaller baitfish.

Bait Jigs do away with baited hooks completely, but they do work a lot better if used in conjunction with berley.

Just about any small baitfish will attack these jigs,. But it is crucial that you use the best size to suit the bait available in the vicinity, keep in mind though that at times bigger fish such as tailor, salmon, bonito and larger mackerel are often about under the smaller targeted baitfish, and occasionally you will be in for some real fun if one takes a smaller sized jig.

WHAT ARE THEY?
Mini lures basically, usually six in total and strung along

Bait jigs are a very effective way of catching bait.

a pre-rigged leader of heavy monofilament line, each of the small flashy jigs is pre-attached to a shortish dropper off the main leader and acts as an attractor to the hungry and feeding baitfish.

The actual jigs come in various sizes and should be selected based on the size of the bait you're targeting, small jigs for herring, pilchards, slimies and yellowtail, and larger for bigger slimies and even small tuna.

SOURCING
There are many different bait jig rigs on the market, and that's because they are incredibly successful at catching bait. Tackle stores generally carry a range of sizes and the price is based on size and complexity of the jigs. For the most part, packets of jigs are expendable, they tangle easily once out of the packet, to the point it often makes sense to reduce the jigs for six to three or four, and the hooks rust and break, but the low price usually means that anglers often don't try and unravel tangled rigs, but simply replace them.

RIGGING
For the most part these rigs come in lengths of 1.5 metres with one end of the leader being joined to the main fishing line via a snap swivel, while the other end is attached to a heavy enough sinker to allow for the rig to be jigged up and down without the jig line bending back on itself and tangling.

When rigging the jig line it is important to make sure that the droppers with jigs attached are standing out from the main leader, if not the jigs won't be effective.

HOW TO FISH BAIT JIGS
Once the bait jig has been correctly attached to the fishing line (using a rod or a handline) you're ready to start catching bait. But as with all

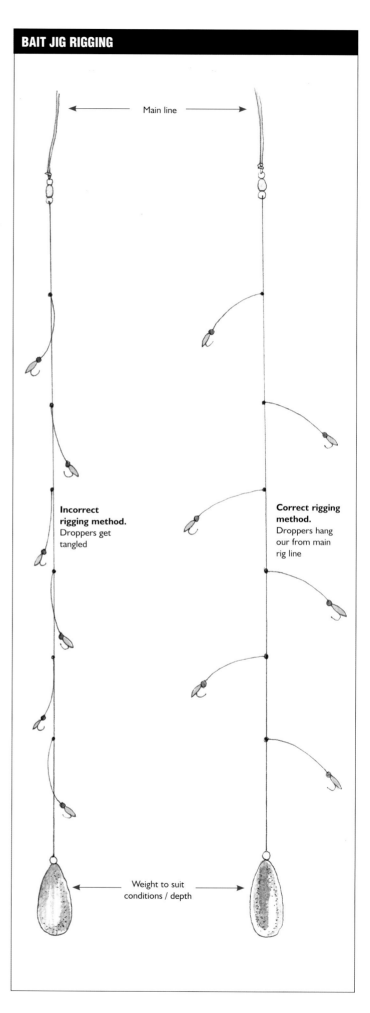

BAIT JIG RIGGING

Main line

Incorrect rigging method.
Droppers get tangled

Correct rigging method.
Droppers hang our from main rig line

Weight to suit conditions / depth

Bait jigs come in a wide variety of sizes.

Nice Kingfish taken on a livebait.

small schooling fish, using berley to attract and hold them where you want them, and to get them excited will pay off handsomely with more fish being caught. It's worth starting to berley as soon as you arrive and before you start rigging up, as this will give the baitfish time to find the berley and mill around.

Once the baitfish are milling around, it's simply a matter of dropping the bait jig rig down to the depth the bait are holding at and a slow up and down jigging motion to get the baitfish biting on the jigs. If you're out in a boat and chasing baitfish, often the up and down rocking of the boat will suffice to impart the jigging action. You'll often find that multiple hook-ups are the norm when the bait are in a frenzy and the bait well will soon be full for the days session.

Don't be afraid to add a small piece of bait to the jigs hooks if the baitfish are being a bit hesitant, this will often be enough to get them feeding and attacking the jig hooks with gusto.

HOW THEY'RE SOLD

Bait jig rigs can be purchased at most tackle stores, and cost between $2 and $6 each, depending on their size and style.

For most anglers who depend on live baits for their fishing and who regularly purchase bait jig rigs, these items are usually regarded as expendable. They tangle badly once unwrapped, and are difficult to store.

Once the hooks — which are weak on most jig rigs — have been broken or rusted, they should be discarded and another couple of rigs purchased to replace them.

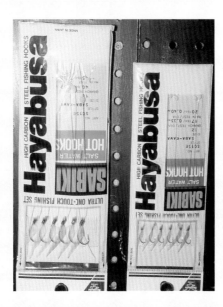

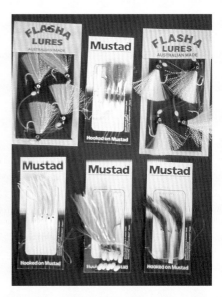

right: Hayabusa bait jigs.
far right: Flasha and Mustad bait jigs.

BAIT COLLECTING GEAR

Clear plastic bait traps are useful for catching mullet and other small bait fish.

This live bait or live shrimp or yabby container can be left in the water or in its matching bucket.

Offshore anglers rely heavily on live baits which they draw to the back of the boat using finely mashed berley.

*H*aving fresh, but especially live bait is one of the key differences between anglers who regularly catch fish, more of them, and bigger and those that don't. Whenever there is a choice, choose fresh live bait. If that isn't possible because of work or location constraints, or bait collecting restrictions, then at least make an effort to buy the freshest bait, be that live or frozen.

Bait collecting can be time consuming, but it can also be fantastic fun, especially with kids in tow who will often get more joy from the collecting of the bait as they will sitting for hours waiting for a bite. If you can store and keep your collected bait fresh, then a day out with the family or mates collecting bait can be a lot of fun and less stressful than rushing to get enough bait while you're thinking about losing valuable fishing time.

KEEP IT LEGAL

Different states have different regulations regarding the collection and use of bait. More and more restrictive regulations are also coming in about where you can and can't collect bait, and catch or possession limits. These regulations have been brought in to protect and preserve various baits and their ecosystems, and it is your responsibility as a responsible angler to know the regulations in the area you're collecting bait and adhere to them.

Remember to try and only take enough bait for your immediate needs, this will not only mean you're using fresh bait, but also helping to preserve bait stocks for future trips and future generations to come.

WHAT TO USE

You can't get more basic than your own hands to collect bait, but a few extra items and tools will help. Collecting fresh bait can often be the easy part, storing and keeping it alive or at least fresh can take far more planning and effort at times.

Pre-planning your bait collecting and bait storage goes a long way towards successful collecting and storage without the waste associated with dead or rotting baits due to poor storage. So the first thing before you head out collecting is to have a storage plan to keep your baits fresh.

Left: A portable live bait tank with attached aerator makes great sense for shore based fishermen.

Below: Live bait tanks are a key component in most fishing boats.

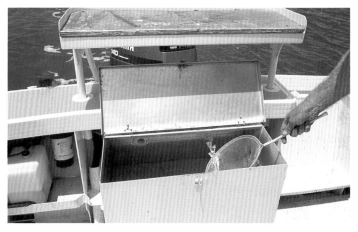

Plastic hand spools or corks can be used to rig lines for bait catching.

Sharp, sturdy knives are an essential part of bait preparation.

PITCH FORK AND SHOVEL

Basic tools for collecting freshwater or saltwater baits can be as simple as a shovel, spade or pitchfork.

These items can be used for collecting earthworms, removing the top layer of debris when searching for bardie grubs, and digging bloodworms across muddy or sandy banks in estuaries.

KNIFE

A sturdy bladed knife is essential for collecting and preparing baits, especially shellfish. But a solid bladed knife should also be accompanied by a selection of other sharp knives for preparing cut baits as well as cleaning caught fish. A multitool knife is also a handy piece of equipment for many uses including fixing bait collecting traps and nets etc when necessary.

As with all tools, they should be maintained in a manner so they can perform as expected, and this is especially so with knives that should be kept sharp.

NETS

Nets of various styles are an important aid to collecting baits, even to the point of small hand nets to catch active grasshoppers! But for the most part, nets are used to collect aquatic insects or often baitfish.

SCOOP NETS

These are generally inexpensive long handled, fine meshed nets used in conjunction with a bright torch or lantern of some type to collect fresh prawns at certain times of the year in shallow estuaries and lakes. The finer the mesh, the smaller the prawn that can be caught. The hardest thing about collecting fresh prawns is deciding whether to use them for bait or a delicious seafood meal!

Scoop nets are also handy for collecting shrimp in weedbeds, simply dragging the net through likely ribbon weed bed areas will often give up good numbers of shrimp, prawns, small baitfish and other possible baits.

These nets can also come in handy for netting small baitfish that can be lured in close with berley around structure and jetties where small baitfish congregate.

DRAG NETS

Where legal, Prawn Drag Nets are a definite aid to collecting good numbers of prawns for use as bait and for the table. They are longer nets that are meant to be used by two people, one on each end, that drag along a stretch of water/shoreline where prawns frequent.

CAST NETS

A circular cone of netting with weights around the perimeter that sink quickly on reaching the water and trap any fish within the net area. The apex of the net has a cord attached and the free end of the cord is attached to the wrist of the caster. The length of the cord is determined by the length of the cast being made. These cast nets take some practise to master, but once you can fold and cast well, they will catch a lot of baitfish such as mullet, garfish, herring and prawns. They are mostly used up north of Australia where larger baits are used live for fish such as barramundi.

BAIT TRAPS

Bait traps can be small clear cylinders with small entrance holes at each end, small baitfish enter to feed on the berley, usually bread, that has been placed inside. Once inside the baitfish are trapped. These bait traps are generally sunk to the bottom around weed areas or structure where the baitfish

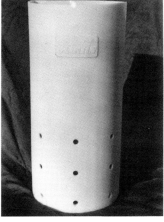

Above: Berley buckets fitted to the stern of boats provide a constant stream of finely choped fish or bread to attract baitfish.

top: Aerators keep live bait swimming by oxygenating water in containers.

centre: Plastic worm pliers can help anglers grasp difficult beach worms.

BAIT COLLECTING GEAR CONT.

congregate, and once on the bottom, the angler also 'seeds' the immediate area with some soaked bread as well to bring the baitfish to the vicinity and get them feeding and drawn to the trap. These bait traps should be constantly worked by the collector, usually 20 to 30 minutes is enough time in the water to start retrieving the trap and collecting the bait. It is important to make sure that the open ends of these funnel traps align with any current flow in the area being trapped.

Other bait traps are made with a metal frame and net mesh, while baitfish seem to be less frightened and caught more regularly in the clear tube traps, both fresh and saltwater shrimp and yabbies, and saltwater crabs are best caught with the mesh traps. These net traps are usually baited with a dead fish frame and placed into the water and lifted regularly to catch fresh bait, or left overnight for collecting fresh the next morning before the start of a fishing session.

BAIT PUMP

If you are constantly using saltwater yabbies, worms and small crabs as bait, then purchasing and learning how to use a bait pump from estuary flats will allow you to catch fresh bait when you want it and save the cost of continually buying fresh bait. These pumps are cylindrical and made from non-rusting materials and work by suction to extract the bait. The bait collector pushes the pump tube down over the yabby or sandworm hole and

NOTE WELL
Certain bait net traps are responsible for the drowning of air breathing native animals such as our iconic platypus, and for this reason, some designs of nets are starting to be banned in southern states.

the plunger handle on the pump is pulled back to suck up the bait, the pump is then quickly extracted and the plunger handle pushed down to extract the sand and hopefully any baits that have also been extracted. If you are collecting baits with these pumps where there is still water across the flats, then you will need to take a circular sieve and rig it up so that it floats. This allows you to work in the water and pump into the sieve, so that the bait is caught in the sieve while the sand filters through.

Bait nets make catching small fish easy.

Bait net loaded with hardyheads ready for use.

Cast nets as shown here take some practise to master, but are well worth the effort.

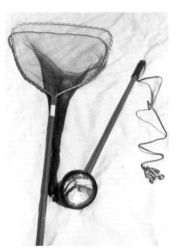
Above & below:
Fine gauge nets can be used for catching shrimp in saltwater and a variety of freshwater baits.

SEA PRO DELUXE FISH COOLER

- Carry Handles • Waterproof Zip
- Fully Sealed • Fish Ruler • 20mm Insulated

DELUXE OMNI BAG

OMNI - 500 mm x 400 mm x 400 mm   AC9072

DELUXE BAG

Small - 750 mm x 400 mm x 200 mm

Keep your catch ICE COOL for LONGER

- Carry Handles • Waterproof Zip
- Fully Sealed • Fish Ruler
- Drain Plug • 20mm Insulated
- 3 sizes available

Medium - 1000 mm x 400 mm x 200 mm

Small	AC8525
Medium	AC8532
Large	AC9058

Large - 1400 mm x 400 mm x 300 mm